William Bradford Dickson

Modern Punctuation

A Book for Stenographers, Typewriter Operators, And Business Men

William Bradford Dickson

Modern Punctuation
A Book for Stenographers, Typewriter Operators, And Business Men

ISBN/EAN: 9783744645843

Printed in Europe, USA, Canada, Australia, Japan

Cover: Foto ©Andreas Hilbeck / pixelio.de

More available books at **www.hansebooks.com**

STENOGRAPHERS, TYPEWRITER OPERATORS

AND BUSINESS MEN

WITH

HINTS TO LETTER-WRITERS, ONE HUNDRED SUGGESTIONS TO TYPEWRITER
OPERATORS, A LIST OF COMMON ABBREVIATIONS WITH DEFINI-
TIONS, AND A VOCABULARY OF BUSINESS AND TECHNICAL
TERMS, WITH SPACES FOR WRITING IN
THE SHORTHAND EQUIVALENTS

BY

WILLIAM BRADFORD DICKSON

G. P. PUTNAM'S SONS

NEW YORK   LONDON
27 West Twenty-third St.   24 Bedford St., Strand

The Knickerbocker Press

1900

Electrotyped, Printed, and Bound by
The Knickerbocker Press, New York
G. P. Putnam's Sons

This little volume is respectfully dedicated to all earnest workers in the World of Commerce, and to all willing students who desire to excel, with the sincere wish that it may prove a help to raise the standard of proficiency in the Art of Punctuation in both the Commercial and Stenographic World.

THE AUTHOR.

PREFACE.

IN this work it has been the aim of the author to treat the art of punctuation as a matter of common sense, good judgment, and taste.

No specific laws or rules are laid down, but modern improved methods of punctuation are set forth in a simple and plain statement of facts,—easily understood and absorbed by the average mind.

While it is true that the illustrative examples in this work are taken entirely from the terminology and phraseology of the business world, this fact in no way limits, but rather enhances, the general value and usefulness of the work.

It has been the experience of the author that many people who have been carefully drilled in the grammatical and rhetorical punctuation of literary language have found themselves unable to practically apply the same rules and experience to the proper punctuation of ordinary business language, whereas many students and printers who have thoroughly mastered the correct punctuation of commercial language have been able to successfully apply, with little or no difficulty, the same principles to the proper division of literary language.

The reason for this lies in the fact that a thorough understanding of the meaning and application of the terminology and phraseology of the business world seems to lead up naturally to a keener appreciation of the value and meaning of literary terminology and phraseology of the literary world, while a thorough knowledge of the use and meaning of literary expressions alone seldom reflects an equivalent amount of light into the mystery of business language.

It is often the case that the merest novice will comprehend and master the technicalities of the business world quite as well as the lettered student.

This book, then, while serving as a guide to correct punctuation for stenographers, business men, and copyists, should also prove of value to those desiring a general knowledge of the art.

It is a work planned to meet the necessities not only of special classes, but of all classes, and as such the author launches it into the busy world, hoping that it may prove an easy, simple, and safe guide to all who desire proficiency in the art of punctuation.

THE AUTHOR.

CONTENTS.

MODERN PUNCTUATION

INTRODUCTORY

WHEN the population of the world consisted of a few wandering nomadic tribes, following their flocks and herds over the hill-tops and through the valleys of the earth, language was in its infancy, and man's vocabulary contained only those words which were the names of absolute necessities,—such as *meat, drink, sleep,* etc. These name-words, or noun-words as they were afterwards known, together with a few simple and natural connectives,—such as *and, to, if, on, or,* etc.,—made up the sum total of his vocabulary.

Then, long-sentence making and paragraphing were unknown. Words were few, sentences the embodiment of simplicity,—brevity the soul of expression. Doubtless man's first sentences were as simple as, *I have come ; I will go ; I will fish ; I will hunt.* As regards simplicity, even the longest sentences of those days were not more complex than the longest sentences in the First Readers of this generation.

At this period of his history, man had little need of punctuation, for the natural pause in his voice after uttering a simple sentence conveyed a sense of completeness to his listeners. Later on, he learned to express ideas through the medium of signs or writing, and at once experienced the need of some sign to indicate the completion of a sentence. He realized that this sign must, in some way, equal in value and correspond to the *voice-pause.*

The simplest sign that occurred to him was, the dash, — the long dash answering the purpose of the period; the short dash that of the comma. Writers of that time had little need of the semicolon or colon, as the relative value of words and phrases did not require its use. Primitive and simple as these methods were, who can say they were not almost as good as our present system of rules, which few understand, though many claim to, but do not?

As time slipped away, man obeyed the natural law of progression, and his sphere of observation widened. He discovered more unknown territory, encountered and mastered deeper relations between objects, and, naming his new discoveries and relations, added new words to his vocabulary. Each century saw the birth of a multitude of new words; and with the growth of words came the growth of sentences, both in length and complexity. With this growth in complexity came a host of *indistinct* relations between words and phrases, requiring greater effort on the part of readers to comprehend written language. Sentences grew so long that they could not be easily understood on first reading unless the mind paused here and there to review the ground, and to consider each individual idea as expressed and its relation to the sentence as a whole. It was self-evident that the mind must be rested here and there in order to understand the meaning of the sentence and appreciate the value of each idea. Suitable signs must be found to represent these rests or pauses : and the signs must be chosen with taste and good judgment. Such were the conditions which made our present system of punctuation an absolute necessity.

There was a time in the history of literature when full, round, long sentences were considered the height of refined and intellectual composition. As the science of literature advanced. however, and by extensive experience writers acquired a knowledge of the effect of sentences of different lengths, it was discovered that it was well-nigh an impossibility to make a long, complex sentence express ideas as clearly and forcibly as medium or short ones. In these days, the forcible and successful writer is the one who expresses himself in medium or short sentences, with a long sentence thrown in here and there for the sake of variety. There are still, however, many writers who use long and difficult sentences, wherein modifying or restricting clauses are not connected with the expressions they are intended to modify, relations dimly indicated, and ideas jumbled up in such a manner as to embarrass and confuse the reader. It is on such sentences that the intelligent punctuator must demonstrate the practicability of his art.

It is well to remark here, however, that the aim of the majority of business as well as literary men is to express themselves in sentences as brief as possible, thus presenting their ideas to the reader in such manner that the mind realizes their importance and force without particular effort.

As the art of written expression grows more scientific, the art of punctuation becomes less important. Much of its necessity will fade with the decline of writers of long, straggling, weak

;entences. The writer who expresses himself simply, briefly, and to the point has comparatively little use for marks of punctuation other than the period and comma, while the long-sentence maker is constantly in need of the art of punctuation to render his meaning clear. Punctuation is declining in quantity and increasing in quality.

The object of this little work is to give the student some practical advice in regard to the use of the comma, period, semicolon, colon, and other marks of punctuation, as well as a number of good reasons for their use. It is not intended as a complete epitome of our present system of punctuation, containing a long list of arbitrary rules. It is simply a plain statement of facts, giving practical reasons for the use of the various punctuation marks, and, as such, has a peculiar value of its own.

Students in our schools and colleges have been drilled in the arbitrary rules of punctuation, but have never been given one tenth the *practice* necessary to make the art of real value. The *reasonableness* of the study has never been placed before them. The usual plan is to have the student commit a system of rules to memory, and send him out into the business or literary world to punctuate as best he can according to his understanding of the subject matter, and the dictates of common-sense.

If the student cannot comprehend the exact meaning of what he tries to punctuate, all the arbitrary rules in the world will not enable him to punctuate correctly. This forcibly demonstrates the fact that arbitrary rules or laws of any kind are perfectly useless, unless the student has a thorough conception of their foundation and meaning, and a perfect knowledge of their proper application. In presenting a work of this nature it is much better, therefore, to appeal to the common reasoning powers of the student, and teach him according to reason instead of rule.

The student must always bear in mind that he cannot become proficient in the art of punctuation (for it is an art), without a vast amount of practice. Theoretical knowledge of a law is one thing, and the adaptation of the same to secure practical results, quite another. The compositors employed on standard publications throughout the world are constantly analyzing the sentences of different writers, inserting commas, semicolons, periods, etc., here and there throughout their productions; consequently many of them are the best punctuators in the world. They become perfectly familiar with the style, the choice of words, and the disposition of phrases and clauses of the various literary people throughout the country, thus demonstrating the truth that continued practice is the only practical road to a thorough mastery of the art of punctuation.

The student must analyze sentences of all kinds over and over again, paying particular attention to the sense expressed therein. He will thus discover the reason underlying the disposition of the different marks of punctuation used in each sentence. After the ground has been repeatedly gone over according to these methods, punctuation will become entirely mechanical,—in fact a mere instinct.

Some people are naturally quick of perception and understanding, and absorb the meaning of a sentence without particular effort. Such people punctuate correctly, although their knowledge of the general laws of punctuation is limited. They have a very vague idea of the value of the comma, the semicolon, the colon, and the period, knowing them simply as signs indicating a certain amount of pause; but their conception of the relation of the various ideas expressed in a sentence is so clear, that they are able to dispose of the marks of punctuation with good judgment and taste. Such people may be termed *natural* punctuators. The majority of people, however, are compelled to give punctuation constant study and practice, in order to become thoroughly accurate in the art.

Many literary men, ministers, and lecturers are poor punctuators. This results from the fact that they take it for granted that anyone who reads their productions can understand the ideas expressed as well as they do themselves. This is the common fault of many writers, and one for which the printer suffers. Many newspapers and periodicals nowadays, however, will not accept an article unless gotten up in neat form, and punctuated perfectly.

The stenographer has no one to look over his work and revise his punctuation. It must come fresh from the machine without a single inaccuracy ; hence the necessity of stenographers being good punctuators. Without proper punctuation a business letter may lose much of its force and importance, and oftentimes may even be misconstrued owing to certain of the sentences being made ambiguous through inaccurate punctuation.

There are many business men who are able to dictate a concise, clear, and well expressed letter, but who have given little attention to punctuation. They expect their stenographers to do it for them.

DEFINITIONS.

A **sign** is the expression of a thought by means of a visible object or action.

As in railroading, different colored lights express different meanings to the engineer ; so, in punctuation, different shaped signs express different relations between words.

Punctuation is a system of rules for the correct division of written discourse by the use of special signs, its object being to aid the reader to a correct understanding of the thought expressed.

Too much punctuation often makes the sense of an article more obscure than too little. Incorrect punctuation indicates that the writer is not clear in his conception of the meaning of the sentence, that he does not quite understand what he is punctuating. How, then, can an incorrect punctuator expect the reader to comprehend readily what he does not clearly understand himself ?

Marks of punctuation may be used according to grammatical law, with grammatical exactness. They may also be disposed of according to the dictates of common-sense, that is to say, by a simple realization of the relation of words, such as

9

might be expected from any person of average mental capacity.

The signs used in punctuation are the Comma, Semicolon, Colon, Period, Paragraph, Interrogation Mark, Exclamation Point, Dash, Apostrophe, Hyphen, Quotation Marks, Parentheses, Brackets, Ditto Marks, and Leaders.

The comma denotes a slight degree of separation ; a semicolon a degree slightly greater than the comma ; a colon a degree somewhat greater than the semicolon ; while the period denotes a full stop, or the termination of a complete thought, —generally speaking, the end of a sentence. The common acceptation of the value of the different marks of punctuation is as follows : The semicolon is equivalent to two commas ; the colon to four commas ; the period to six commas ; in other words, this proportion represents the relative amount of pause indicated by each sign.

NOTE.

Only the *minor* marks of punctuation, such as can be explained and disposed of by a short definition or a few remarks, are handled under the above head.

The more important marks of punctuation, the Comma, Semicolon, Colon and Period, are each given a complete chapter immediately following.

The Paragraph expresses a degree of separation greater than the period or any mark of punctuation, and denotes the introduction of a new subject or a direct change in thought.

A paragraph should embody a collection of thoughts upon one particular subject. If it is long and involves the thought expressed on two or more different subjects, even though they may be slightly related, the distinction between them is less marked and it is more difficult for the reader to realize the force and importance of each. Paragraphs, then, should never be longer than necessity demands.

In dictating a business letter, the dictator is apt to dilate upon three or four different subjects. Some of these subjects will be slightly related to each other while the rest of them will bear no relation whatever. All the various ideas expressed upon each particular subject should be grouped in the form of a paragraph. Frequently it will require considerable judgment on the part of the stenographer to decide this matter, but continual practice will make the art of paragraphing an easy accomplishment.

Paragraphic writers on the different papers throughout the world are men who have choice thoughts on various subjects of particular interest to the public. Such writers always arrange their thoughts in an effective manner, grouping them in the form of a paragraph. Short paragraphs are always more effective than long ones, because the reader is enabled to retain nearly all the thought expressed.

The Interrogation Mark designates the termination of a direct question ; thus,—"Can you do anything by that route ? Do you guarantee quality of goods you quote ?"

The Exclamation Point, in its general use, designates the termination of an expression of wonder or surprise. In the commercial world, however, its principal uses are to denote emphasis and to express irony or contempt ; thus,—" An Unparalleled Offer !" is an example of the use of the exclamation point for emphasis ; while, " Selling out below cost ! Who could believe such an advertisement !" expresses irony.

In the following example it is evident the exclamation point is used to express irony :

Your explanation, which is replete with sound reasoning, (!) proves you to be a great (!) salesman, remarkably adapted to this business.

The interrogation mark also is frequently used to express ridicule, irony, and contempt ; thus, " What a remarkable (?) man he is."

The Dash is used to denote a sudden change in thought or an omission of letters. In some instances it is used to separate parenthetical expressions from the rest of the sentence. The dash is frequently used in connection with the colon to indicate a slight increase in the degree of separation expressed by the colon. It is also used with

the comma for the same purpose. A comma and
dash are about equivalent to a semicolon, while a
colon and dash express nearly the same amount of
pause as the period.

We also send you two copies of a new catalogue gotten up in
good form,—one to put in your register or other convenient
place, and the other to keep in your pocket.

Glass Works.—We will accept 1151, Kansas City Glass
Works.

You will notice that on all desirable business we have largely
increased our lines,—a policy that we think will make the
company valuable to you.

The terms offered by the company are most liberal :—a
commission of five per cent. will be paid,—that is—$50 per
$1,000 ; and it is not unlikely that you could make from $50
to $500 a day for several weeks.

We have your favor of the 31st ultimo, and note what you
say in regard to policy number 764,824—Elton.

764,917—Harrison. We note what you say touching same.

The fact of his knowing contents of package, which is identical with those you have, excepting that you claim the package, when received, contained but a coat and vest—pantaloons
missing,—is sufficient proof of his ownership.

F——54——M——206.

September——6——'84.

Dear Sir,—Dear Sir :—

As follows ;—As follows,—As follows :—2d ed.—pp. 167-8.

S. of the Cor. of Sec. 27—11-25.

The Apostrophe is used to denote the omission of letters in contractions and abbreviations ; thus, *don't, can't, mang'r.*

It is also used before a final *s* to signify possession ; thus, " John's investment " ; " Henderson's disbursements."

When the word denoting possession ends with *s*, or is plural in form or by nature, the apostrophe follows instead of precedes the *s ;* thus, *Mr. Williams' property ; Karges' store : for goodness' sake.*

EXAMPLES.

A slight decline in Boyton's saws has taken place.

Your account has now been credited $15 on Winslow's Soothing Syrup, as per your card of the second.

January 25', '89.

Invs't, Dep't, Bld'ng, Att'y.

The apostrophe is frequently used to denote dimensions ; thus,

6 feet 4 inches may be expressed, 6' 4".

The Hyphen is used to connect two members of a compound word ; to show proper syllabication of a word at the end of a line ; to connect firm-names which are compounded. It is also used to compound familiar terms which from constant use have attained the import of one word.

EXAMPLES ILLUSTRATING USE OF HYPHEN.

Freight-claim—department-voucher.

Gill-Alexander Electric Co.

Weir-Shugart Implement Co.

Herald-Chronicle.

Co-operation.

We have just secured a new line of ecru and tan shades, 11-12 twill, 40-inch, all-wool French cashmere.

We have a small quantity of 40-inch, all-wool albatross.

We are also out of square Japan fans and all sizes in low-price Japanese folding-fans.

Our plan is to send notices to all policy-holders.

The colors include black, seal-brown, navy-blue, cardinal, green, tan-brown, cream, garnet, and wood-brown.

We regret exceedingly the non-delivery of your esteemed order.

Left-hand wood-beam plows.

2 ⅛-inch steel tubular axle, equal to 3 ¼-inch thimble-skein bed-brake wagons.

The nine-hoe drill is worth $12.

The above buggies have A wheels, 28-oz. machine-buffed leather quarters and back-stays.

Wood-box, ice-house.

Twenty-one, forty-two, fifty-five, etc.

The tendency of modern times, however, is to eliminate the hyphen as much as possible. Many words which were formerly written in their compound form are now written as one word ; such as shorthand, typewriting, warehouse, etc.

Quotation Marks denote the introduction into written or printed discourse of the exact words or thought of another ; thus,

We have your telegram saying, "Ship the goods immediately," and have obeyed your instructions.

Quotations may be divided into two kinds,— direct and indirect :

A direct quotation is the exact words of another, and an indirect quotation the expression of another's words in your own language ; thus,

He wired us, "Ship two cars No. 2 red wheat," is a direct quotation, while "he wired us to ship him two cars of No. 2 red wheat," is the indirect quotation for the same expression. Quotation marks should be used to denote direct quotations only.

Parentheses are used to separate parenthetical and explanatory expressions from the main sentence ; thus,

Collin's axes and picks reduced 50 cents in list. (This in addition to reduction advised last month.)

Our rule concerning this matter as given in clause 12 of the Special Instructions (Superintendent's transfer report), is as follows :

On Wednesday last (4th inst.) to avoid delay, we entered the bark *Northern Light* in the name of the Railroad Company.

(See chapter on Parenthetical Expression.)

Brackets are of the same general nature as parentheses, but are used to enclose a note, explanation, or correction ; thus, Softly falls [fall] the shades of evening.

Ditto Marks are used to indicate the repetition of an expression which occurs in a preceding line ; thus,

The assets of the business, real and nominal, are as follows :
New York real estate, unincumbered.......$20,000,
New Jersey "   "   "   16,000,
Westchester "   "   "   .... 6,000.

Leaders are dotted lines which direct the eye from the name of a commodity to its quoted price ; thus,

Rye... 95,
Bran.. 98,
Winter wheat................................. 98,
No. 2 red wheat.............................. 93.

Leaders are also used to denote the omission of names or dates, designating the place in written or printed matter where a name or date has been omitted and is to be inserted afterwards ; thus,

....................189 ......
Policy No............Name of insured.................
In witness whereof I have hereunto set my hand............
day of...... ....189 ....
2

USES OF THE COMMA.

The comma signifies different degrees of pause according to the position it occupies, or the use to which it is put. It is the most frequent and important signal in the art of punctuation, and has seven well established values.

The different values of the comma, named in the order of their importance, are as follows : to denote an omission ; to indicate the termination of a preparatory expression ; to indicate a modifier set away from what it modifies ; to separate parenthetical expressions from the main sentence ; to separate different members of a long sentence ; to introduce a short quotation ; to separate a series of words or phrases.

OMISSIONS.

Unnecessary expressions are always eliminated from business letters. This necessitates the omission of such familiar words or phrases as the writer deems should be easily understood by the reader. Whenever such omissions occur, the comma is used to indicate a short pause, during which the reader is supposed to supply mentally the omitted word or phrase. In every case the omitted portion is an unimportant word or phrase which is easily understood, and which does not particularly affect the sense of the sentence.

EXAMPLES OF OMISSIONS.

Enclosed find check for $50, amount of our account in full.

We will sell you these goods for $1.25, 5 %, four months from January first.

We shall be glad to have you make us an offer of, say, $5.60, sight draft, with bill of lading attached, delivered at Buffalo in five or ten car-load lots.

We have a copy of your reply under date of 27th ult., in which you stated to Messrs. M. & N. that the purchase of January, February, March, English shipment, is equivalent to a March, April, and May delivery, 30 days.

UNIMPORTANT OMISSIONS.

Some omissions are so unimportant that it is unnecessary to indicate them by a comma. In the clause, " Herewith find check for $10," there is an omission of *you will*, between the words *herewith* and *find ;* but this omission is so easily understood that the reader does not find it necessary to pause even a single moment to supply it. There are many similar examples in business correspondence of all kinds, and the writer must use considerable judgment as to whether or not an omission is important enough to be indicated by a comma. Most omissions are not.

PREPARATORY EXPRESSIONS.

Any word, phrase, or clause, which precedes a sentence and indicates both by its *form and meaning* that the main clause is to follow, may be called a preparatory expression. These expressions never make complete sense in themselves, but are so worded as to lead up to and introduce the main assertion ; thus,

Carefully considering your proposition of the 10th, we have come to the conclusion it would be better for you to forward the goods immediately.

The use of preparatory expressions is considered a very strong feature of commercial language, for the reason that every preparatory expression not only represents a thought of its own which is more or less related to the main thought, but expresses it in such a manner as to attract the attention of the reader and make him understand that there is something important to follow : that which does follow is always the main idea which the writer wishes to put forth.

The comma should be used at the end of every preparatory expression. Its office is to give the reader time to absorb the sense of the preparatory expression, to prepare himself for the main assertion, and to note the relation existing between the idea expressed in the preparatory expression and the thought brought out by the main assertion.

CONDITIONAL CLAUSES.

A conditional clause is one which implies a condition, that condition being related in some way to the main clause. It is of the same nature as the preparatory clause and might be classed as a conditional preparatory clause ; thus,

If the goods are not too much damaged, we will accept them and make shipment at once.

Nearly every business letter begins with a preparatory clause and has in the body of it one or more conditional clauses. Preparatory clauses usually begin with participles or words of similar importance ; such as, *awaiting, hoping, notwithstanding, trusting, fearing, feeling, replying ;* while conditional clauses begin with words or phrases implying a doubt or condition ; such as, *if, perhaps, it may be,* etc. Conditional and preparatory clauses, however, are similar in construction and closely related.

Preparatory expressions may be divided into three classes, *i. e.,*

Preparatory expressions of the first class, or introductory words.

Preparatory expressions of the second class, or

introductory phrases or clauses ; as, " On your invoice of the 19th, you called for 10,000 feet of long leaf yellow pine."

Preparatory expressions of the third class, or complete sentences ; as,

Referring to your letter of the 21st inst., wherein we stated to you that you had overcharged us on this invoice, we again call your attention to the fact that we can not afford to lose this amount.

EXAMPLES OF CONDITIONAL AND PREPARATORY CLAUSES.

Awaiting reply and hoping to be favored with your orders, we are,

Trusting we may be favored with your orders, we remain,

Replying to yours of the 6th, we beg to say that if the S. S. S. is in good condition, we have no objection to taking it back.

Should you be able to buy another lot of these goods at 4 cts. per yard, we have no doubt that we can place it.

Concerning the question of payment of duties at Baltimore, we wish, as in the past, to use every endeavor to dispatch your business.

Referring to your letter of May 12th to E. S. Barrett, our attorney, in relation to the crossing in the city of Topeka, would say, that before receiving the former notice from you, I directed the Division Superintendent to fix up this crossing. Should any of the others now be in poor condition, if you will kindly advise me what the trouble is, I will see that they are repaired without further delay.

In the meantime, you will take no further notice of the matter, but go on and do the work on the ground.

As the seven cars you received have been unloaded, it is impossible to again check the lengths and numbers of the rails.

Unless the goods are delivered by the 16th inst. at the very latest, I cannot receive them, as after that date they will be perfectly useless.

In the present condition of trade, we cannot take the risk of ocean freights.

If, therefore, Mr. Vauze is not entirely satisfied with his adjustment, he is at liberty to return the same.

MODIFYING OR RESTRICTING CLAUSE OUT OF ITS PROPER POSITION.

When a business man is working under high pressure and his brain is in a turmoil with ideas seeking to get themselves expressed, he is very apt to construct a sentence which will fairly indicate the state of his mind. In other words, he will form long sentences wherein modifying clauses, which may express ideas of considerable importance, will be set at some distance from what they are intended to modify. It takes all the skill of the writer to separate these restricting clauses in such manner that they may be clearly comprehended by the reader at first reading.

A modifying or restricting clause out of its direct position or relation should always be preceded by a comma, in order that the reader may pause, quickly review the sentence, and definitely ascertain to what expression the modifier belongs.

Sometimes a slight change in the punctuation of such a sentence will make it mean something entirely different from what the dictator intended it should. On this point the writer should be very careful and clearly understand the dictator, being sure that he knows what the dictator intended to say. It is sometimes best entirely to reconstruct a sentence filled with ambiguous modifiers, instead of endeavoring to punctuate it.

EXAMPLES.

We quote you $4.35 per ton for old rails, subject to your immediate acceptance by wire.

We have observed with some care the tendency shown by some jobbers to cut prices, owing chiefly to the active competition.

We shall be pleased to have your quotations on corn from time to time, as may suit your convenience, and perhaps same may lead to business.

Please search your records covering different ways it may have to come to you, or of being disposed of, and advise.

The goods you shipped have arrived, but we are not prepared to put them on the market, as it is a little too early in the season, but will do so in the course of a month.

PARENTHETICAL EXPRESSIONS.

A word, phrase, clause, or sentence suddenly introduced into any part of a complete sentence, is called a parenthetical expression. It is an intruding thought which interrupts the sense or natural connection of words, but which serves more or less to explain or qualify the principal assertion ; as, " Will you oblige us, confidentially, with information relative to this firm." In this sentence the chief thought is, " Will you oblige us with information relative to this firm," but after the originator of the sentence had conceived the complete thought, a new idea entered his mind, and that idea was that the information had better be confidential ; so, when he gives verbal expression to his sentence, he introduces the new thought in the midst of the sentence.

While this thought is more or less an intrusion and has no special grammatical connection with the rest of the sentence, it very materially affects the sense, making the sentence much stronger and more important.

HOW DIVIDED.

. Parenthetical expressions may be divided into two kinds and three classes.

The kinds are as follows :

First. Parenthetical expressions which relate directly to the sense of the sentence and which cannot be omitted without particularly affecting its importance and force. The example given above is a parenthetical expression of this nature.

Second. Parenthetical expressions which are

directly related to the sense of the sentence and
may be omitted without particularly affecting the
importance or force of a sentence ; thus,

" Will you acquaint us, as far as lies in your power, with an
exact statement of his affairs."

The classes are as follows :
Parenthetical expressions of the first class, or
single words or short phrases ; as,

" We have sent you ten copies of our large edition (mounted)
of the revised rules of interchange."

Parenthetical expressions of the second class, or
complete phrases and clauses ; thus,

" I call your attention to Mr. Cline's letter of the 24th and
mine of this date (copies of both herewith) in reply to yours of
the 7th."

Parenthetical expressions of the third class, or
complete sentences and even paragraphs ; thus,

" Again the defendant attempts to prove by the witness
John Powell, that the plaintiff, Ed. Powell, paid the sum of
$100 (see Powell's evidence commencing on page 227)."

HOW SEPARATED.

If directly related to the sense, importance, and
force of a sentence, parenthetical expressions of
the first class should be separated from the main
body of a sentence by commas only. It it has no
particular bearing upon the meaning of the sentence,

such a parenthetical expression should be separated by parentheses. Most parenthetical expressions in business correspondence are related in some way to the sense of the sentence in which they occur, and are separated by commas only.

Parenthetical expressions of the second class, if directly related to the sense of the sentence, should be separated from the main sentence by commas ; if not directly related, by parentheses.

Parenthetical expressions of the third class are usually separated from the main sentence by parentheses, if directly related to the sense of the sentence ; if indirectly, by brackets.

EXAMPLES OF PARENTHETICAL EXPRESSIONS.

The latter, we understand, was a locomotive valve oil.

This, with the hearty co-operation of your customers, will secure to all who handle our goods full and legitimate profits.

In anticipation of the spring and summer trade, now about to commence, we beg to advise you that we have packed largely of the crop, 1884.

These goods should be made a little lighter, say 15 to 16 ounces, as they are for the Southern trade.

The pattern is excellent, as is also the color, but the weight does not meet our approval.

LIST OF PARENTHETICAL EXPRESSIONS.

The following is a list of the most common parenthetical expressions :

Consequently, furthermore, however, indeed, perhaps, also, then, therefore, too, likewise, moreover, nevertheless, accordingly, unquestionably, doubtless, meanwhile, lastly, formerly, namely, of course, in fact, to be sure, no doubt, in general, in reality, in a word, in that case, in the meantime, in the first place, in every respect, for the most part, without doubt, beyond question, now and then, on the contrary, on the other hand, generally speaking, as it were, in short.

LONG SENTENCES.

It frequently happens that a business man carries in mind many ideas bearing upon the same subject, each idea being more or less dependent upon the other for the full expression of its meaning. When he attempts to express these ideas in written form, they are likely to appear upon the paper in the shape of a long compound or complex sentence. This sentence may have two or more members connected by the conjunctions *and*, *but*, or *for*. In such cases these conjunctions should be preceded by a comma, thus dividing the long sentence into its distinctive parts, in order that the reader may be able to comprehend each part, as a part, and determine the relation of the same to the sentence as a whole.

If the sentence is an unusually long one and its different members are already subdivided by a number of commas, it is best to show a greater degree of separation between the parts by using a semicolon before the above mentioned conjunctions, thus giving the reader more time to determine the relation and meaning of ideas.

No effort shall be wanting on my part, not only to do a good business with old customers, but to open up new accounts.

Mr. Jones starts for the west the latter part of this week, and will have the pleasure of seeing you in, say, two weeks' time.

There are various cheaper oils offered as equal to ours, but a trial of them will convince you that they are inferior in every way.

(See first use of Semicolon on following pages.)

QUOTATIONS.

A word, phrase, clause, sentence, or paragraph expressing the exact words of another, used in written or printed discourse for explanation, illustration or example, is called a quotation ; thus,

We have your telegram of to-day which reads, " Ship seven boxes via steamer *White Star*," and have complied with your request.

Another meaning for the word quotation, as used in the commercial world, is the enumeration of commodities with prices attached ; thus,

We quote you as follows :
Dry salt meats, 10 cts.; Choice cull hams, $12\frac{1}{2}$ cts.

Quotations may be divided into two classes.

Quotations of the first class, or short phrases or clauses ; thus,

Yours of the 12th at hand ordering one drum of roasted coffee same quality as that sent you July 23d, with instructions that it must be light, saying, "If it is not light, we can not keep it."

In reply we wired you, "Market busted in No. 2 wheat ; cannot pay more than 68 cents."

Quotations of the second class, or complete sentences ; as,

Mr. Ross wires me under date of 16th as follows ; "There is no contract that in any way, directly or indirectly, affects the established rate on wrought-iron bridge material."

Quotations of the third class, or complete paragraphs—sometimes pages ; thus,

Whenever Mr. Johnson receives a claim for this department, to be checked, he stamps on the original expense-bill :

"This expense-bill does not agree with the records in my office ; see copy of billing attached, etc., etc."

Some quotations consist of a single word or phrase only, and fit into the main sentence so nicely that it is not necessary to introduce them by any mark of punctuation, the only separation necessary being expressed by the quotation marks ; thus,

We are in receipt of samples of "Star," also samples marked "No. 2," sent us some time since.

This iron is to be style known as pattern "J" in your catalogue.

These goods were sold "as are," consequently we can not allow your claim.

If you have some "gilt-edged" hay, we would be pleased to have your order on same.

Quotation marks, like exclamation points and question marks, are sometimes used to express irony or contempt ; thus,

I omitted to state in my letter of Saturday, that probably the origin of the " storm " upon the canal was in the contractors allowing a large boulder to roll into the canal from Campbell's Hill

HOW INTRODUCED.

Quotations of the first class, that is, short quotations not exceeding a line in length, should be introduced by commas.

Quotations of the second class, or quotations over one line in length and not exceeding two lines, should be introduced by semicolons.

Quotations of the third class, or quotations consisting of whole paragraphs or pages, should be introduced by a colon and a new paragraph.

The office of the comma in introducing short and medium quotations is identical with the use of the comma at the end of preparatory expressions ;

it indicates a short pause in order that the reader
may realize the import of the sentence which introduces the quotation, prepare himself for the quotation which follows, and thoroughly note the
relation between the introductory clause and the
quotation.

EXAMPLES OF QUOTATIONS.

Replying to your telegram of to-day which says, " Ship 12
cars No. 2 wheat to-day," we have this to say :

We wired you yesterday, " Hold goods for further orders,"
and now confirm same.

In regard to delivery they telegraphed as follows ; " We will
fill the contract within 60 days, but may send the first car-load
next week."

I am in receipt of the following, under date of June 1st, from
Mr. Kerr :
" Mr. Beech has shown me Mr. Palmer's letter to him of
Saturday last, in which he says he considers it his duty to
apply for an injunction to stop all work inside of the ten-rod
limit."

A SERIES OF WORDS AND SHORT PHRASES.

In business it is frequently necessary to enumer-
ate a short list of articles, commodities, or particu-
lars of some kind.   In a series of this kind where
the expressions composing the series consist of a
single word or short phrase, such words and phrases
are separated by the comma ; in this instance the

comma denotes the elimination of the co-ordinate conjunction *and*. This use of the comma would be properly classified under the head of omissions, previously explained, but it is awarded a separate heading because of its constant use in this capacity.

EXAMPLES OF A SERIES OF WORDS AND SHORT PHRASES.

During the past month we have received numerous shipments of Rye, Barley, Oats, Corn, and Wheat.

Please send us per Union Line :

25 Boxes raisins,

10 Bbls. currants,

28 Boxes Oswego soap.

3

THE SEMICOLON.

The semicolon has five distinct uses :

1st. Before the conjunctions *and, but, for,* etc., when used to connect two members of a long sentence wherein the members are already subdivided by commas ; thus,

Do we understand you to say that your shipment would be from Buffalo, or from Chicago via Buffalo ; that is, after we give our orders, will we be obliged to wait for the corn to arrive at Buffalo from Chicago?

To you, therefore, I apply in this difficulty ; and should esteem it a great favor if you would acquaint me, as far as lies in your power, with information respecting the character and means of this firm.

With a view of increasing our membership among first-class risks, we have decided to write a limited number of $5,000 policies gratis ; in other words, to waive the usual admission fee of $5.

2d. To separate two members of a short sentence when such members are only slightly related, each member being nearly equivalent to a complete sentence ; thus,

We have it here : letter-day.

The other goods to which you refer, we can let you have at the price you mention ; terms are satisfactory.

3d. To separate a series of expressions composed of phrases, clauses, or short sentences ; thus,

Messrs. Taylor & Co. advise us that the *Ella* is now due at Baltimore, and that she has for you on your order with Taylor & Co., through us, 118 tons No. 1 English Bessemer pig ; 119 tons No. 2 Bessemer pig ; 114 tons No. 3 Bessemer pig.

Please buy the following laces :
1 piece very fine Valenciennes ; 8 pieces Honiton ; 10 pieces best Irish Point ; 10 pieces white Yak Lace ; 8 pieces

4th. Before *as, viz., to-wit, namely, i. e.,* followed by examples or illustrations ; thus,

In reply to your favor of the 20", we quote you buggies at the lowest possible prices ; viz. :

A grade buggies....................$65.00,
B   "   " 60.00,
C   "   "   ....65.00.

5th. Before *and, but,* and *for*, when these conjunctions are used to introduce a final clause for the purpose of contrast or explanation ; thus,

This is certainly not the result of the use of our oil ; but it is no doubt caused by impurities in the water which you used.

I do not desire it renewed, as I will have no use for it ; but I fear that it may fall into improper hands, therefore notify you to have it taken up.

THE COLON.

The colon has four distinct uses :

1st. To separate two members of a very long sentence, already subdivided by commas or semicolons ; thus,

You may return the 11 pairs of French Kids to us by express ; or, if you can sell them at a discount, you may do so : but bear in mind that we do not know just what the discount should be ; still we will make you an allowance of 25 cents per pair.

It is well to remark here that this is a very infrequent use of the colon in business language. Nowadays sentences are seldom made so long and straggling as the example given above.

2d. To separate clauses complete in themselves, possessing the attributes of a full sentence, yet related to each other by the sense expressed ; thus,

Send us your late catalogue : we are in the market for your goods.

In the above example the colon denotes the omission of the conjunction.

3d. To introduce a long quotation. Probably its most frequent use is after the phrase " as follows," when introducing long business quotations wherein are given the names of articles with prices attached ; thus,

We are pleased to quote you special prices on our goods as follows :

Anthracite coal................$9.00 per ton,
Bituminous " .... 6.00   "   "

The colon is commonly used after the expression " Dear Sir " ; sometimes after sub-headings.

4th. To introduce :

1. A long explanatory sentence or paragraph ; thus,

My idea about the matter is this : that before the end of the year these lots could be sold at a fair profit, and thus you would be released from paying anything further on them.

2. A long business proposition ; thus,

I will make this further proposition to you : that if you will make the $600 payment on these lots, I will take one half interest with you, by assuming and paying interest on $800 of the purchase money, to be secured in two notes, each for $500.

3. A long business statement ; thus,

Relative to this matter I will make the following statement : that on the 29th of September we shipped the wheat from various stations on the C. & A. R. R., and supposed, of course, that it reached you promptly at the expiration of the allotted time.

The office of the colon in the examples above given is identical with that of the colon when used

12758

to introduce a long quotation. In these instances the colon expresses a considerable amount of introductory pause before the explanation, proposition, and statement, in order that the reader may prepare himself to fully appreciate their value.

THE PERIOD.

The period is used to denote the termination of a complete sentence; also after headings, sub-headings, signatures, addresses, abbreviations, etc.

The office of the period is so naturally and commonly understood that it is unnecessary to illustrate its uses by examples.

The period should never be used after *st*, *d*, *th*, when used in connection with numerals.

ABBREVIATIONS.

Abbreviations may be divided into two classes ; first, complete abbreviations, which are always denoted by the period ; thus, Mr., Mrs., Dr.

Second, partial abbreviations, or those in which a small portion of the word is omitted, this omission being denoted by the apostrophe ; thus Man'g'r, Sec'y.

The following list of contractions and abbreviations includes the greater portion of the frequently recurring ones now in use in the commercial world.

A PARTIAL LIST OF ABBREVIATIONS.

A. B.   Able-bodied seaman. (*Artium Baccalaureus*) Bachelor of Arts [see B. A.].
Abp.   Archbishop.
A. C.   Army Corps.
Acc., or acct.   Account.
A. D.   (*Anno Domini*) In the year of our Lord.
Ad., or Adv.   Adverb, Advertisement.
A. D. C.   Aid-de-camp.
Admr.   Administrator, administration.
Admx.   Administratrix.
Ad v.   (*Ad valorem*) At the value.
Agr.   Agriculture.

Agt. Agent.
A. M. (*Artium Magister*) Master of Arts [see M. A.].
(*Ante meridiem*) Before noon.
Amt. Amount.
Anat. Anatomy.
Anon. Anonymous.
Ans. Answer.
Apl. April.
A pri. (*A priori*) Beforehand.
Art. Article.
Atty. Gen. Attorney-General.
Aug. August.
Ave. Avenue.

B. A. Bachelor of Arts [see A. B.].
Bal. Balance.
B., Bbl. Barrel, barrels.
B. B. Bill book.
B. C. Before Christ.
Biog. Biography.
Bk. Book, Bank.
B. L. Bachelor of Laws.
B/L. (Also written B. L.) Bill of lading.
Bl., or Bls. Barrel, barrels.
Bot. Bought.
Boul. Boulevard.
Brig. Gen. Brigadier-General.
Bro. Brother.
B/S. Bill of Sale.
Bu., or Bush. Bushel, bushels.

C. B. Cash book, Companion of the Bath.
C. C. County commissioner.
C. C. P. Court of Common Pleas.
C. E. Civil engineer, case excepted.
C. F. I. Cost, freight, insurance.

Chap. Chapter, Chaplain.
Chf. Chief.
Cin. Cincinnati.
C. J. Chief Justice.
C. L. Car load.
Clk. Clerk.
Co. Company.
C. O. D. Collect (or cash) on delivery.
Coll. College.
Cor. Corner.
C. P. Common Pleas, Court of Probate.
C. R. Carrier's risk.
Cr. Credit.
Crim. con. Criminal conversation, or adultery.
C. S. Court of Sessions.
Csh. Cash.
Cshr. Cashier.
Cts. Cents.
Cwt. Hundredweight.

D. C. L. Doctor of Civil (or Canon) Law.
D. D. (*Divinitatis Doctor*) Doctor of Divinity.
Dec. December.
Dft. Defendant.
Deg. Degree.
Dep. Depot, Deposit.
Dept. Department.
D. H. Deadhead.
Disct. Discount.
Dist. District.
Dist. Atty. District Attorney.
Div. Division.
Dr. Doctor.

E. B. Expense bill.
Ed. Edition, editor.

E. E.   Errors excepted.

E. N. E.   East-northeast.

Eng.   England, engine.

Encyc.   Encyclopædia.

E. O. E.   Errors and omissions excepted.

Esq.   Esquire.

Et al.   (*Et alii*, or *aliæ*) And others.

Etc.   (*Et cætera*) And so forth.

Et seq.   (*Et sequentia*) And following.

Et ux.   (*Et uxor*) And wife.

Ex rel.   (*Ex relatio*) At the relation of.

Fahr.   Fahrenheit.

F. B.   Freight bill.

Feb.   February.

F. O. B.   Free on board.

For.   Foreign.

Frt.   Freight.

Ft.   Fort, foot, feet.

Gal.   Gallon.

G. A. R.   Grand Army of the Republic.

Gov.   Governor.

Hab. corp.   (*Habeas Corpus*) You may have the body.

Hab. fa. poss.   (*Habere facias possessionem*) A writ to put the plaintiff in possession.

Hab. fa. seis.   (*Habere facias seisenam*) A writ now superseded by the preceding.

Hhd.   Hogshead.

Hon.   Honorable, Honorary.

Ib., or Ibid.   (*Ibidem*) In the same place.

Ictus.   (*Iurisconsultus*) Counsellor-at-law.

I. e.   (*Id est*) That is.

In.   Inch.

Inc., or incor.   Incorporated.

Incog. (*Incognito*) Unknown.
Inf. (*Infra*) Beneath or below.
In f. (*In fine*) At the end of the title, law, or paragraph quoted.
Inst. Instant.
Int. Interest.
I. q. (*Idem quod*) The same as.

J. Judge, justice.
J. A. Judge-Advocate.
Jan. January.
J. P. Justice of the Peace.
J. Prob. Judge of Probate.
Jr. Junior.

K. B. King's Bench, Knight of the Bath.
K. C. B. Knight Commander of the Bath.
Km. Kilometre (metric system).

L., or £. (*Libra*) A pound sterling.
Lb. or Lbs. (*Libra, libræ*) Pound, pounds.
L. c. Lower case (printing).
L. C. J. Lord Chief-Justice.
L. C. L. Less than car-load.
Lieut., or Lt. Lieutenant.
Lit. D. (*Literarum Doctor*) Doctor of Letters.
LL. B. (*Legum Baccalaureus*) Bachelor of Laws [see B. L.].
LL. D. (*Legum Doctor*) Doctor of Laws.
LL. M. (*Legum Magister*) Master of Laws.
Loc. cit. (*Loco citato*) In the place cited.
Lon. Longitude.
L. S. (*Locus Sigilli*) Place of the seal.

M., or Mons. (*Monsieur*) Sir, Mister.
M. A. Master of Arts [see A. M.].
Mag. Magazine.

Mar. March.
Max. Maximum.
M. C. Member of Congress.
M. D. (*Medicinæ Doctor*) Doctor of Medicine.
Mdlle. Mademoiselle.
Mdse. Merchandise.
Mem. Memorandum.
Min. Minimum.
Messrs. Messieurs.
M. P. Member of Parliament
MS., MSS. Manuscript, manuscripts.
Mo. Month, Missouri.
Mr. Mister.
Mrs. Mistress.
Mt. Mount.

Nat. Natural, National.
Nem. con. (*Nemine contradicente*) No one contradicting, unanimously.
Nem. diss. (*Nemine dissentiente*) No one dissenting, unanimously.
N. L. (*Non liquet*) It does not appear; the case is not clear.
N. North.
N. N. E. North-northeast.
N. N. W. North-northwest.
N. W. Northwest.
No. Number.
Nol. pros. (*Nolle prosequi*) Unwilling to prosecute.
Non con. Not content.
Non cul. (*Non culpabilis*) Not guilty.
Non pros. (*Non prosequitur*) He does not prosecute.
Non seq. (*Non sequitur*) It does not follow.
Nov. November.

O. C. Overcharge.

Oct.   October.
O. K.   All correct ; all right.
O. R.   Owner's risk.
O. T.   On track.
Oz.   Ounce.

¶.   Paragraph, Page.
Pcs.   Pieces.
Per an.   (*Per annum*) By the year.
Pd.   Paid.
Pkg.   Package.
Plff.   Plaintiff.
P.M.   (*Post meridiem*) Afternoon.
Pm't.   Payment.
Pp.   Pages.
Prof.   Professor.
Pro tem.   (*Pro tempore*) For the time being.
Prox.   (*Proximo*) Next (next month).
P.S.   (*Post scriptum*) Postscript.

Q.   Question.
Qt., qts.   Quart, quarts.
Q. V.   (*Quod vide*) Which see. (*Quantum vis*) As much as
    you please.
Qy.   Query.

Rec.   Recorder.
Recd.   Received.
Recpt.   Receipt.
Rep.   Representative, Report.
Rev.   Reverend.
R. R.   Railroad.
R'y.   Railway.

Sci. fa.   (*Scire facias*) Make known.
S. E.   Southeast.

Scil., or **Sc.**, or **Ss.** (*Scilicet*) That is to say, to wit, namely.
Sec. Section, Secretary.
Sec'y. Secretary.
Shp't. Shipment.
S. J. C. Supreme Judicial Court.
Soc. Society.
Sol. Gen. Solicitor-General.
Sq. Square.
Sq. ft. Square feet.
Sr. Senior.
S. S. E. South-southeast.
S. S. W. South-southwest
S. W. Southwest.

Ter. Territory.

Ult. (*Ultimo*) Last (last month).
U. P. Upper Canada.
U. S. (*Ut supra*) As above.

V. Verse.
Vat. Vatican.
Vid. (*Vide*) See.
Viz. (*Videlicit*) Namely.
Vol. volume.
Vs. (*Versus*) Against.

W. West.
Whf. Wharf.
W. N. W. West-northwest.
W. S. W. West-southwest.
Wt. Weight.

Yd. Yard.
Yr. Year.

REMARKS.

Among modern business men there is a tendency
to eliminate the period after many of the constantly
occurring abbreviations, such as, *inst, ult, prox.*
Probably the time is not far distant when the period
will be considered an unnecessary part of all abbreviations, since an abbreviation is known by its general form rather than by the period following ; in
other words, every abbreviation has some peculiarity
of its own which enables the reader to tell it at
sight. The period following does not materially aid
him in determining what the abbreviation represents,
if he has not previously been instructed as to its
meaning.

Abbreviations should never appear in the body of
a letter. The student will find by experience that in
most instances it is about as easy to write out the
full word upon the machine as to abbreviate it.
Abbreviations are not conducive to neatness, ele-
gance, and completeness in typewritten matter.

GENERAL INSTRUCTIONS.

The following examples have been selected with considerable care and are intended to illustrate the different uses of the various marks of punctuation. In order to thoroughly master the marks of punctuation as disposed of in these examples, the student should work according to the following method ; copy the sentence given below upon the typewriter, omitting all marks of punctuation ; then with pencil carefully punctuate every example according to preceding rules and instructions, studiously comparing your work, after finishing, with the punctuation as given in the examples, in order that you may determine where you have fallen into error.

· Continue this method of practice until you are able to punctuate all the following examples correctly. You are then ready to continue the study of punctuation from business letters after the same method as given above, *i. e.*, choose an important letter from some standard letter-book, such as *Humphrey's Manual*, *Payne's Business Letters*, etc., and copy the letter upon the typewriter, carefully giving it the proper form but omitting all marks of punctuation ; then with pencil punctuate this letter to the best of your ability, according to preceding rules ; then compare your punctuation with that given in the book and correct : continue this method for a few weeks and you will punctuate as well as the best.

In *How to Become Expert in Typewriting*, Mrs. Arthur J. Barnes lays down the following valuable plan for gaining proficiency in punctuation. The student will do well to follow these instructions implicitly. It is undoubtedly the most practical method known.

" Write a letter three or four times with all the punctuation dictated to you. Write the same again from dictation supplying all of the punctuation yourself. Compare your work with the print and note all errors in punctuation, etc. If you have made mistakes write it again. If not, take something new. This practice will give you the facility in writing from dictation and will also teach you how to punctuate correctly. In a short time it will enable you to punctuate a letter well and without help the first time you typewrite it from dictation. It will also add greatly to your speed."

PROMISCUOUS EXAMPLES.

It appears the package in question was shipped the day after the one which you received, and the clerk there, happening to write your entry first, and the names being so much alike, thought, of course, they were one and the same item, and accordingly sent us a tracer for your package without looking further.

Yours of the 7th inst is at hand, and I must say that we are indebted to you for setting us on the right track, and must also apologize for the annoyance you were put to concerning a package belonging to another party.

In relation to this matter, would say that we find to have way-billed in all seven boxes to same parties on the same date ; and, as we are unable to determine which one of said numbers is the box in question, we would suggest that you have a search made of your records.

This done, you can easily learn whether box from H. B. & Co. was or was not included in the seven boxes.

We have sent to your house on three different occasions to obtain a package, but so far have been unsuccessful.

I am pleased to learn that you have closed with Fox Bros. for 1000 barrels of molasses and 500 sugar Shooks at 20 cents, shipped to pay differential duty ; and I hope you will be able to close with Lord & High for the empties.

Still, rather than lose them, I would take them at 70 cents, if we cannot obtain them at a better figure.

Our commission on this car was a small one ; but, under the circumstances, you may deduct 50 cents per ton from the invoice, as the shipment was delayed somewhat by the mill.

Your car of oats is probably shipped before this, but we have no advice as yet ; it ought to reach you in a short time.

It costs 6 cents per hundred freight, or about 2 cents per bushel, making them cost you 44-2 there.

This is really better for you than buying goods in this market at $4.45, plus freight and cartage, independent of which you receive unassorted stock instead of assorted.

We enclose you herewith, sample of our No. 900 Broadcloth, of which we have had an enormous sale, it being largely used for ladies' suits, ladies' and children's jackets, wraps, etc.

We have given a great deal of attention to the manufacturing of these oils, supplying, as we do, the largest works in the United States.

Enclosed please find affidavit of car of oats No. 371, shipped to Rhinebeck, April 1st, short less 10 per cent., ten bushels.

We regret the extraordinary delay in the arrival of your flour, and will try to see to it that these delays do not occur again.

Would not be surprised if the car reached you in one or two days, but to make the matter sure, send you twenty barrels to-day.

This wagon has 1 1-2 inch axles and wheels, bed 8 feet 4 inches long, 3 feet 6 inches wide ; capacity 1500 pounds.

The gear is painted straw color ; body wine color.

This wagon we quote you, with flare boards and brake, $112.50.

Will send sample in a day or two ; have none on hand at present.

We credit your account with $100 on last 100 bushels of oats as requested, and hope same will be satisfactory.

The empties, when received, will be duly credited to your account ; in the meantime will ship, as directed, five gallons like the last.

Enclosed find check for $46.90, in payment of bill for 55 empty oil barrels, and blank receipt, which please sign and return.

We are entirely out of size 32 at the price you named ; have size 317.

Note what you say about 8-2 dozen flannel shirts, lot 317, which were duly received to-day.

We have not the particular shade ordered, so send you the next best in different shades, not knowing that you wished them for a club.

We have decided to close out this season and, to accomplish this, will sell to you at 10 1-2 cents, next 60 days, for 25 piece lots ; 11 1-2 cents, regular to select.

Russell & Erwin announce change of discount to 50 and 2 per cent., and alter lists.

We are advised by Calkins & Co., of the charter of sailer *Gia Comino*, with 590 tons iron rail ; also steamer *Belsize*, with 5,000 tons scrap iron.

We called to-day on the Edgar Thompson Steel Co., for the purpose of selling the remaining 500 tons, which we proposed to do, delivered at Baltimore ; but while they are disposed to take the iron, they are not willing to accept delivery at Baltimore, and insist upon our delivering it at Bessemer, or no sale.

The writer is under the impression that Mr. Wilson has already sent you request to have all rail ends received for our account, classified as per our standard, that is, in five classes ·

Double heads over 20 inches long, short ends 9 inches long ; lumps, to make fifth class.

This was based on our rate of 8 cents per one hundred pounds to Pittsburg, which, of course, does not include switching charges.

In reply we quote you 20 pound T iron rails, first quality, at 3 cents per pound, F. O. B. cars, Wheeling, West Virginia.

The present rate of freight to Detroit, all rail, is 17 cents ; rail and lake, 12 cents.

I have been in correspondence with them about it and Mr. Ross wires me under date of 16th as follows : " There is no contract that in any way, directly or indirectly, affects the established rate on wrought-iron bridge material."

In my opinion, it is not possible for the C. B. & Q. people to determine in case of complaint, whether any contract is in violation of the agreement ; that, it seems to me, is the right of judgment accorded to ourselves.

The matter was brought to my notice in this way : A man named Anson who sells second-hand machines, called us up over the telephone and asked us if the machine was sold.

The market was somewhat less active this forenoon, but prices, which were regular at the opening, were well maintained.

Pacific Mail was the exception to the rule, the price dropping at length to 51, a decline in the last three days of about 10 per cent.

As the seven cars you received have been unloaded, it is impossible to again check the number and lengths of the rails, and I must take the invoice as corrected ; and, in so doing, have to charge you with 645 rails instead of the number mentioned by you, 644.

The cars numbered 6789 and 4573, on original invoice, and which you have not unloaded, are, as per telegram to-day, to be returned, and I have so advised our road master.

It is returned to you to-day, by express, for repairs.

Please fill in the name of the agent to whom you desire the policies mentioned in the accompanying schedule transferred ; see that the names of the insured are immediately entered upon his collection book, and the collection promptly attended to ; then return the schedule to this office.

On procuring Mr. Eckert's acknowledgment for moneys received, you will be kind enough to insure regularity, to compare his signature with that previously transmitted to you.

Soliciting the continuance of confidence heretofore reposed in us, we remain,

Yours respectfully,

By way of reference, I beg to state that I was for many years assistant and manager of the house of Messrs. Dodge & Co., to whom I am at liberty to refer you for information respecting my habits, character, etc.

Should you feel disposed to receive my orders and to place me on a footing similar to that of my predecessor, I trust that we may have the pleasure of doing business together, resulting in mutual profit and advantage.

Replying to your inquiry of the 5th, we quote you our " Favorite " shellers as follows :

Without fan or feed table..............$5.75,
With table 6.00,
With fan and feed table............... 6.50.

Replying to your inquiry of the 5th, we quote you our " Favorite " shellers as follows :

Without fan and feed table, $5.75,
With table,   6.00,
With fan and feed table,   6.50.

Replying to your inquiry of the 5th, we quote you our "Favorite" shellers as follows:

Without fan and feed table	at	$5.75,
With table	at	6.00,
With fan and feed table	at	6.50.

Following please find car-load sales to-day : Cooper & Co., one car, Oxford, Ala., 25,000 pounds dry salt cribs, loose, 7 1-2 cents.

Please forward as soon as possible, the articles detailed in the enclosed list ; and if, as I doubt not, the goods come up to my expectations, I hope to have the pleasure of extending my relations with your house.

The following rate will be in effect from November 1st, 1884, to March 31st, 1885, inclusive :

By agreement of the Standard Committee of the Joint Executive Committee, the present basis of rates on articles named below, viz., 20 cents per one hundred pounds, Chicago to New York, may be granted for the year ending Dec. 1st, 1885.

Referring to Joint Executive Circular No. 475, "Basis of Investment-bond Rates to Sundry Western Points," issued April 11th, 1883,

Notice has been received from Mr. A. G. Blair, G. F. A., Wheeling and Lake Erie, and Cleveland and Marietta Railroads, that, on and after February 1st, 1885, those roads will require their local traffic rates from junction points to the following local stations on west-bound traffic :

Circular No. 687,—Joint Executive Committee.

W. H. Powers, Passenger Agent,
W. St. L. & P. R. R.,
Toledo, Ohio.

W. H. Powers, Esq.,
Passenger Agent, W. St. L. & P. R. R.,
Toledo, Ohio.

C. H. Carpenter, Genr'l Pasng'r Ag't,
G. T. R. R.,
Kansas City, Mo.

Replying to your favor of the 7th, we cannot accept your offer at the price named, nor can we accept the terms.

We are now closing out our stock of spring and summer shawls at greatly reduced prices, and invite your special attention to this department.

Thanking you for your past favors, and soliciting a continuance of same, we are, gentlemen,

Had we known it yesterday, I think we could have obtained a better price from Adams.

I am very much pleased with your good work in loading this vessel so rapidly, and hope you have been able to clear her to-day, as intimated in the telegram from Mitchell this morning.

We feel that we are doing as well, if not better, than some of the commission houses handling these goods.

Appreciating past favors, we remain, Dear Sirs,
Yours faithfully,

EXPERIMENTAL EXAMPLES.

After giving the following examples very careful study as to the correct punctuation, take a sharp pencil and accurately insert all marks of punctuation where they belong ; then have some person dictate them to you upon the typewriter. Do not allow the dictator to assist you in the work by suggesting or reading the marks of punctuation, but punctuate to the best of your ability as you go along. After having gone through all the experimental examples in this way, compare your machine work with your pencil work, and see if you have succeeded in punctuating the examples exactly as you did with pencil. Have these examples dictated to you upon the machine several times, continuing the work until you can take them easily and punctuate them accurately without the slightest hesitation.

Please ship to the Kansas City D P & R R Co care of M K McIntyre Kansas City Mo Via K C N D R R the articles specified below and send bills for same direct to this office in duplicate without fail

The above will make one car load this to be shipped at once

subject to inspection at Kansas City if you cannot fill the order at once return to me by first mail

We have given your account credit for 600 feet in the short in car 15564 amounting to $14.40 subject to being allowed by the shipper

Your invoice of June 23d for car 736 we have just checked over and find you have made a slight error in the extension of feet

Rye is worth 22 cts this is with the supposition that the grain is dry and in good condition for shipping

I have your letter in the matter of rates on packing house products from Wichita and Hutchinson and note particularly your justification for the re-adjustment

All of the above cars were reported in bad order in Central R R yards at Columbus Ga November 15'h also K C S & M box car 476 which was delivered to you by K C M & B August 22d reported in Columbus yards a total wreck November 15th

Please buy the following ribbons and send them per U S express white moire ribbon

3 pieces No 2   3 pieces No 4   2 pieces No 7

Please buy the following muslins Lonsdale Fruit of the loom Pride of the West Waumsetta Chapman all bleached.

Replying to yours of the 5th we wired you as follows we price you No 27 Eureka outfit complete as you describe at $335 60 days or $350 contract terms $18 back freight we have it here letter to-day

Should it be that we are owing this amount the same would not be due before the date October 12th and would not commence to mature until November 27th

When the coal department makes a bill against your department for coal furnished stations etc you ascertain from Division
Supt where the coal has been received writing them a letter in
this form

Referring to your letter of the 28th which is in answer to my
letter of May 15th indicating to you settlement we proposed
and did make in claim No B 631 I have this to say

The reason given by the clerk who wrote the letter dated
June 25th why the Frisco should not join us in this claim was
no reason at all

Referring to attached papers we shall be glad if you will tell
us at once the reason for the delay in transportation of car in
question

We are unable to tell whether the date of your letter of Jan
21st is 7 or 9 it looks to us like a nine

We are at present out of the 24 by 36 pound Clifton manilla
we can send you 35 at once or we can back order and ship the
30 pound on arrival of the stock

We will send you certificates of weights and draw on you at
sight with invoices and bill of lading attached

In harrows we have the Scotch at $4 the three section 45
tooth harrow at $5 the three section wood reversible at $10 and
the three section steel reversible at $11

We have now received information from the Bain Wagon Co
and we can quote you the freight wagons for which you made
inquiry as follows

Hope you will be able to capture this order and promising
if you do so to get the goods as promptly as possible we are

Such wheat as you sent us a sample of is worth 90 cts at your
place if dry

No 29 is worth on track your station 56 delivered here this week 57 and 58

Your letter of the 11th making inquiry concerning the matter of jewelers safe with chest inside also as to the matter of time on 57 safe has just come in and we wired you "yes" to both of your inquiries which we presume will explain the whole matter

Will you kindly favor us with your opinion of the financial responsibility character etc of R H Jones and Company giving us as far as you know such facts as to how much they are supposed to be worth and whether they have any real estate in their name in your city or elsewhere thanking you in advance and promising to reciprocate when called upon I am

H R Williamson Division Superintendent Armstrong Kansas

W T Newman Purchasing Agent Rialto Building Chicago Ill

W K Lambert District Supt N Y Life B'ld'g St Louis Mo.

R F Woodard Division Supt Denver Col

W T Vance Esq Assistant Master Mechanic Holdon Mo

W H Warren Master Mechanic St Louis Mo

W B Wilson Supt Atchison Kansas

Martin Cook & Leipeser 73 Woodard St N Y

Direct a number of envelopes, using above addresses, giving each address its proper form.

SUGGESTIONS TO TYPEWRITER OPER-ATORS.

1. Accuracy first, speed afterwards.

2. Evenness of touch is the prime requisite for beautiful work.

3. Carry in mind the following thoughts : correct form ; evenness of touch ; accuracy ; neatness ; speed.

4. Learn to use every finger on each hand as soon as possible, then practise "touch method" until you can operate the machine without looking at the key-board.

5. Strike the marks of punctuation with the little finger.

6. Cultivate your touch until you can strike the period gently enough to prevent it from puncturing the paper.

7. Follow the instructions given below on entering the office each morning and continue faithfully until they are fixed habits.

   1. Clean the carriage and the body of the machine with a soft rag.

   2. Use a long-handled brush and dust all parts which cannot be reached by the hand.

3. Clean the back rod ; oil the front rod.

4. Brush the face of the type thoroughly with a stiff brush.

5. Adjust your ribbon from one spool to the other, so that it will run all day without attention, also adjust it so that the type will strike in a new place.

6. Index the letter book.

8. Never touch any adjustments on the machine unless absolutely necessary. A machine wears itself so as to work smoothly to certain adjustments. If the slightest change is made, the machine does not respond to action nearly so well.

9. Always keep ribbon rests on the machine to prevent the ribbon from curling and sagging.

10. Keep a neat bright cover close at hand to throw over your machine when obliged to leave it for a short time.

11. Always use the ribbon reel in putting on ribbons.

12. Keep an old pair of kid gloves handy in order to protect your hands when changing ribbons or cleaning the machine.

13. You should have in your machine drawer :

1. A stiff brush for cleaning type.

2. A long-handled soft brush for dusting machine.

3. A small oil-can containing a supply of the best machine oil.

4. A box of nickel polish.

5. A large soft cloth and a chamois skin.

6. A small screw driver.

7. A few extra rubber bands for the type-writer.

8. An old pair of kid gloves.

9. Some small-sized rubber bands.

10. An envelope and postal-card guide.

14. It is a good plan to keep both a purple copying ribbon and a black record ribbon on the machine.

15. A good method for thoroughly committing the key-board to memory is as follows : Cut some thin paper in small discs just large enough to fit the top of a key, then paste one of these over the " E " and one over the " A " key the first day : One over the " P " and one over the " Y " key the next day, and so on until you are operating a key-board of blanks. You will then be able to throw a hand-kerchief over the key-board and operate it without difficulty.

16. Whenever you get in a hurry you are liable to get in trouble.

17. The ability to make perfect letter-press copies is one of the chief requisites of office work.

18. Do not speak to your employer unless it is absolutely necessary.

19. Speed can best be attained by the continuous re-writing of the same letter or circular. Choose a

representative six- or eight-line letter or circular and write it at least 1000 times.

20. Always address an envelope for each letter.

21. Never sign a letter unless requested to do so.

22. Be sure to get the proper enclosures in each letter

23. Whenever there are any enclosures to be made, mark on the lower left hand corner of the letter, before taking it from the machine, " one E.," " two E.," etc., according to the number of enclosures to be inserted.

24. Be sure that all envelopes are correctly addressed : many a stenographer has lost his position through no other fault than addressing envelopes incorrectly.

25. Avoid as much as possible asking your employer for explanations, or to repeat what he has dictated. Of course explanations are in order at times, but make them as few and far between as possible.

26. When copying exceedingly important work, always use a line marker to avoid all possibility of losing or transposing a line.

27. Do not work without a copyholder of some kind.

28. Always have on hand a scratcher and a rubber eraser also, but use them as little as possible.

29. Never put a pencil or a pen correction on your typewritten work.

30. Practise the art of making beautiful copies upon the Mimeograph and other duplicating devices

31. Always operate your machine with the lightest finger tension possible.

32. Use the finger movement entirely when operating the machine.

33. If your machine jars each time the carriage spaces your carriage tension is too tight.

34. Make yourself thoroughly competent before entering an office, even if it takes a year ; then ask for your true value.

35. Make yourself familiar with every kind and quality of paper on the market, and learn to choose paper suitable to the work which is to be done ; also determine what kind of paper will produce the best results.

36. Make yourself familiar with all kinds, qualities, and colors of ribbons on the market.

37. Be willing to do any reasonable amount of work outside of your profession ; you may be an expert, but no business firm can afford to let you remain idle. Get a good salary, then work for it.

38. You will always find good fresh air, beautiful outlook, and lots of room on the top round of the ladder.

39. Practise tabulating on the machine until you can do it neatly and accurately.

40. Use good judgment as to when to use double and single space.

41. When a mark of punctuation occurs before a direct quotation, the punctuation mark should be struck first, then the quotation mark. If a punctuation mark occurs at the end of a direct quotation, the rule will hold good.

42. Never remove paper from rear of the machine.

43. Be careful about your syllabication at the end of a line. Inaccurate syllabication denotes carelessness and ignorance.

44 Do not cramp or curve your fingers while operating ; keep them as nearly straight as possible.

45. Cultivate the ability to take in long sentences. Don't be a " bobber," *i. e.*, one who bobs his head from his notes to the machine every few words.

46. Practise writing on ruled lines so you can do so easily when occasion requires.

47. Cultivate a sharp, quick, sudden, but delicate stroke : do not hammer.

48. Practise making duplicates with carbon paper until you can do it neatly and accurately.

49. If you cannot spell, do not call yourself a stenographer until you can.

50. In your odd moments look up the principal shipping points adjacent to your city.

51. Use abbreviations as little as possible.

52. Keep at hand a package of pins, some different-sized paper fasteners, a bottle of mucilage, and some manuscript covers.

53. File away each day's answered letters early the following morning.

54. A dim ribbon can sometimes be made to do better work by turning it under side up.

55. Practise putting on rubber bands until you can do it quickly.

56. Practice taking dictation on the machine until you can do such work accurately and rapidly.

57. In contracts and important documents give all amounts both their written and numerical form ; thus, twenty-five dollars ($25). In ordinary business letters the numerical form will do ; thus, $25.00, or $25.

58. Always use an envelope guide when directing a large number of envelopes.

59. Always try to repair your own machine as quickly as possible, but do not spend too much time over it ; rather send for the regular repairer.

60. You cannot successfully re-ink an old ribbon.

61. Buy your ribbons by the half dozen or dozen.

62. Set your standard so high that if you fail you will still be above the average, even in failure.

63. Remember you cannot confine the world to one system of shorthand or typewriting, or one make of typewriter, any more than you can stop Niagara ; still, you want the best.

64. Be careful to have your back partially to the light when operating the typewriter ; at night be sure to have the machine directly *under* the light.

65. Know your machine; give its mechanical construction careful study so you will know the office of each part.

66. Practise designs for ornamentation so that when occasion requires you can do such work.

67. Hold down the space bar and *before releasing it* strike lower case " c," and the left oblique fractional dash (/) and you will have a suitable character for the word " cents " ; thus, 50¢.

68 Do not space between parentheses and the expression they enclosed.

69. Do not make a space either before or after a hyphen.

70. When a letter occupies one full page and over always head the next page with the initials of the party or firm to whom you are writing, the number of the page, and the date of the letter.

71. Be careful not to get ribbon stains on key tops.

72. Sapolio will remove ribbon stains from the fingers.

73. Put a darning needle or a match in the cork of the oil bottle. The eye of the needle or the end of the match will take up enough oil to use on any part of the machine.

74. An exclamation point can be made with the colon and the apostrophe.

75. Use the quotation marks and apostrophe to express feet, inches, and seconds ; thus 6 ft., 6 in. equals 6' 6".

76. When writing a telegram, never divide a word at the end of a line.

77. When writing single space between lines, use double space between paragraphs.

78. Do a little more work than you are paid for and you will get your dues by and by.

79. To make a continuous line upon the typewriter hold the hyphen lightly against the paper and push carriage back and forth a few times.

80. The use of a period after an abbreviation does not prevent the use of another point immediately after it.

81. Leaders are made by a continuous striking of the period or dash.

82. The ability to operate the typewriter without looking at the key-board, will save you four hours out of eight, as it permits the eye to rest continuously on the copy.

83. You should train your little finger to hold down the upper case key.

84. Small " L " may be used to express *one*, and capital " O " the *cipher*.

85. Point off large sums or amounts into divisions of three figures.

86. Fractions may be expressed in two ways, 3/4, 3-4 ; the latter being most common.

87. Do no scratching, erasing, or " Xing " if possible to avoid it ; but if absolutely necessary to erase, first scratch the paper slightly with a knife,

then use the best quality of rubber eraser afterwards Select a rubber full of grit.

88. You can make no erasures in carbon work ; all errors must be " Xed " ; thus, XXX.

89. Write the body of a telegram or cablegram in capitals.

90. Benzine may be used to clean type and soften thick oil on different parts of the machine.

91. Teach yourself to strike a type key and the upper-case key at the same moment, and make a perfect capital.

92. In figuring the number of words on a page, count 12 words to each line and multiply by the number of lines.

93. An operator furnishing his own machine should receive compensation at a higher proportionate rate.

94. A word written in capitals attracts more attention than an underlined word. Capitals, to secure attention ; underscored words for emphasis.

95. Take some standard shorthand magazine such as the *Phonographic World*, the *National Stenographer*, etc.

96. Buy some practical work on typewriting *Touch Writing*, *Practical Typewriting*, *How to Become Expert in Typewriting*, are the best.

97. Buy some standard work on letter writing, such as, *Humphrey's Manual.*

98. Buy a book called *100 Valuable Suggestions to Shorthand Writers.*

99. The Centering Scale given below will prove a valuable aid in quickly determining centering points.

Count the number of letters and spaces in the heading which you wish to place in center of page, then refer to scale below. If your heading has 12 letters and spaces in it, you would begin at either 26 or 27 on the scale ; if your heading has 41 spaces and letters in it, you would begin at 12 on the scale ; if your heading has 18 letters and spaces in it you would begin at either 23 or 24 on the scale, etc.

CENTERING SCALE.

1—32	17—24	33—16	49—8
3—31	19—23	35—15	51—7
5—30	21—22	37—14	53—6
7—29	23—21	39—13	55—5
9—28	25—20	41—12	57—4
11—27	27—19	43—11	59—3
13—26	29—18	45—10	61—2
15—25	31—17	47— 9	63—1

100. Always address the envelope before commencing a letter.

101. Be strictly confidential : do not allow an outsider to read a half finished letter in the machine.

102. In invoicing capitalize articles given.

1. Always omit a comma rather than put it in the wrong place.

2. Make an effort to know where commas belong, then put them there.

3. Be sure of your spelling; leave nothing in doubt.

4 In writing " My dear Sir," capitalize *My* and *Sir*, but not *dear*. In writing " Dear Sir " capitalize both words ; in " Very respectfully," etc., capitalize only the first word.

5. Do not write the sign for "and" (&) except in Company or firm names.

6. Never write Co. for *Company* in the body of a letter.

7. Never put a period after 1st, 2d, 3d, 4th, etc., nor after Miss.

8. Never contract the word Messieurs into Mess.; always use Messrs.

9. When expressing No. 1, No. 2, No. 3, etc., always use No. for the word *number* and the figures for the actual number, as shown.

10. Always write dates in figures.

11. Avoid abbreviations in the body of a letter.

HABITS OF BUSINESS.

1. Industry.   3. Calculation. 5. Punctuality.
2. Arrangement. 4. Prudence.   6. Perseverance.

"WHAT IS PUNCTUATION?"

"If a man thinks in crisp sentences he will punctuate with semicolons; if he has a pure epigrammatic style of composition he will employ more periods than other points.   If his sentences are long and involved he will use commas; if interrogative, interrogations; if ambiguous, parentheses, so it may be said that we punctuate as we feel.   Not as *we* feel that *somebody else feels*, not in the sense that *another* would imply, but in our *own sense* of what *we* would imply in using the same words that another uses to express an idea."

SYLLABICATION AND PRONUNCIATION.

Few stenographers realize the importance of giving the above-named subjects the proper time and attention. Nothing indicates such complete ignorance of word construction as inaccurate and faulty syllabication at the end of a line. Amanuenses should take great care to make a thorough study of syllabication in order that all words may be correctly divided. The vocabulary of business terms given at the end of this book will enable the student to master the proper syllabication of many of the commercial terms in use.

As regards pronunciation, the study of this art will do more to make you accurate in spelling than any other study outside of syllabication. It is almost impossible to find a person who has given proper attention to syllabication and pronunciation, who cannot spell accurately.

In studying a word with reference to its proper syllables and the proper sounding of each syllable (or pronunciation), the student naturally absorbs, along with this study, a correct concept of the proper spelling of the word, and this without appar-

75

ent effort on his part. To master a word as it should be mastered, implies the following :

First : A correct idea of the letters used in the construction of that word.

Second : A thorough knowledge of the syllables into which these letters may be divided.

Third : A correct knowledge of the proper sounding of these syllables, or pronunciation.

Fourth : A complete knowledge of the various definitions belonging to these words.

Fifth : A thorough knowledge of the general use and application of the word (which implies a mastery of the definition most commonly used).

One of the latest and best works on syllabication and pronunciation is Phyfe's *7000 Words Often Mispronou ced*, and the intelligent and ambitious reader who wishes to educate himself thoroughly in the right direction cannot well afford to be without Phyfe's work, which can be used profitably in connection with this volume.

LIST OF BUSINESS AND TECHNICAL TERMS.

In order to use this vocabulary of words effectively, the student should work according to the following plan :

Beginning with the first word, commit to memory the correct spelling for the first twenty words ; repeated practice by writing them out in their correct form upon the typewriter, or in longhand, is the best way to secure this result.

Now take Webster's Unabridged, and make a careful study of all the meanings of each word as given therein.

Then use each of the twenty words in business sentences of your own construction, until you have their general position and relation firmly fixed in mind.

By observing this method you will master :

First. The correct spelling.

Second. The exact meaning.

Third. The proper application of every word in the handbook.

Nothing more can be desired.

In compiling this list of words it has been the aim of the author to encompass only the common terminology of the business world, omitting all exceptional words.

The only true foundation for a student to build upon is a thorough mastery of the simple and ordinary words of business life, leaving time and experience to gradually develop him in a knowledge of extraordinary and unusual words.

Many of the most common words in every-day life are most difficult of formation in shorthand, and present the most awkward outlines ; hence a second reason for introducing so many short and familiar words. The student will find the shorthand analysis of such words of incalculable value to him. He should carefully determine a brief shorthand outline for each word in the list, then fill in this character on the line to the left of each word.

After completing the entire list according to this method, he should then carefully practise each outline until he can execute it readily and read it at sight without the slightest hesitation.

This plan is, of course, applicable to all systems of shorthand.

LIST.

abandonment	accompanying
abatement	accomplice
abduction	accomplish
abeyance	accomplishment
abnormal	accordance
Abraham	accountable
absolutely	accountant
abundance	accredited
abuttals	accretion
accent	accrue
acceptance	accumulate
acceptor	accumulation
accessory	accuracy
accommodate	accurately
accommodation	accuse
accompany	accustomed

79

	acknowledge	— ·	administering
—	acknowledging	——	administration
——	acknowledgment	—··	administrator
———	acquaint	—— ·	adoption
	acquaintance	——	*ad valorem*
	acquiesce	· ——	advancement
—	acquiescence	— ——	advantageous
—	acquire	—— ·	advantageously
—	acquit	————	advertise
—	*acta*	———	advertisement
—	activity	———	advertising
—	acuteness	——— ··	advisability
—— ·	adapted	— —	advisable
—·	additional	——	advisement
—	address	——	affiant
—·	adheres	———	affidavit
—	adjacent	———	affiliation
—	adjourn	——	affirmant
——	adjustment	——	affirmation
——— ·	adjutant	———	affix

affray — alleging

aforesaid — allowance

agencies — alphabet

— agency — alteration

- aggregate — alternate

aggressive — alternative

aggrieve — amanuenses(plural)

- aghast — amanuensis

— agricultural — amass

— agriculturist — ambiguity

— aisle — amenable

Alabama — amendment

— — albatross — amicably

—. albumen — Amsterdam

albuminoids — analysis

alderman — analyze

- *alias* — ancestor

— *alibi* — angle

— alienation — annex

— allegation — announce

	annoyance	——-	appliances
	annual	——— -	application
	annually	——— —	appoint •
—- - — -	annuity	——— —	appointment
	ante	——— -	apportionment
—	anthracite	———	appraisement
	anticipation	———-	appreciate
—	antiseptic	——— - -	appreciating
— -	anxiety	———	appreciation
— ———	anxiously	—— —-	apprentice
————	anybody	———	apprenticeship
——- -	apologize	——	apprise
———	*a priori*	—— -	approaching
———	apparel	———	approbation
— -	apparently	—— —	appropriating
—-—-	appeal	———	appropriation
--	appearance	———	approval
	appellant	—— -	approximate
	appellate	——	appurtenance
	appendant	—— —	arbitration

arbitrator	assessor
architect	assign
architectural	assignee
arisen	assignment
Arizona	assignor
Arkansas	assimilation
arraign	assistance
arrangement	assistant
arrears	associate
arson	association
article	assortment
articulate	assume
asbestos	assurance
ascertain	assuring
asphaltum	attaching
assassination	attainment
assault	attachment
assertion	attempt
assess	attestation
assessment	attorney

———— attract

—— audience

——— authority

·—— authorize

——— automatic

·— autumn

—— auxiliary

——— available

—— — axe

· ··· axis

———— axle

———— backward

—— badge

——— · — baffle

bagatelle

· — ·· baggage

balance

— Balbriggan

— balconies

balustrade

bankrupt

bankruptcy

bargain

— barrel

——— barter

——— basis

———— battery

·—— believe

———— beneficiary

———— benefited

——— benevolence

———— bequeath

———·— berry

—— — Bessemer

——· bias

———···· biblical

——· bigamy

——— bijou

—·· bilious

———	billiard	-	box
———	birthday		brandy
———	biscuit	——-	— bribery
———	bitumen		bristle
—— ——	bituminous	— .. -	Britannia
- —- ——	blackmail		broadcast
.- ——.	*blasé*		broadcloth
.-	bleached		brokerage
—	Bohemian		Brussels
—	bologna		brutality
—- ..	bolster		bud
—	*bona fide*	_	buff
——- —-	bonanza		bulletin
—	bondholder		bullion
—	bonus		buoyancy
	bookkeeper		burdensome
...	bookkeeping		buried
———	boss		bury
———	boulder	—— —— —	bustle
———	bowlder	———	business

	busy	capabilities
		capacity
	cablegram	⁚— ‥ — capias
-	calculate	‥—‥ ‒ capita
—	calculating	—‑‑ capital
	calendar	—— capitalist
	calender (press)	capitol (building)
	California	‑—— ‧ carcass
— ——	calorific	——‑‑ cardinal
—‑‑‑ ‑	cambist	carefully
——	Canadian	‥—— cargo
—‑‑—	canal	— ‥‑‑ ‑ carriage
—	cancel	‑— ‧ carrier
—	cancellation	‑— *carte-blanche*
—	candidate	———— cashier
	cannel	— —‑ cashmere
	canon	‑ catalogue
	canvas (cloth)	———— caterer
—	canvass	—— ‥—— caveat
—	canvasser	——‑ cement

censured	———— chimney
central	—·——— chinchilla
centre	—— · chisel
ceremony	—— ·· · choose
certificate	—— chudda
certify	— ···· church
chafing	———— ·· circle
challenge	—— circular
champagne	· ——— circumstance
channel	— ·——· circumstantial
character	··· citation
characteristic	··· cites
chargeable	· citizen
chattel	· civility
chattel mortgage	claimant
cheat	·· ·—— claim department
check	———·· classification
chef-d'œuvre	———— classify
chemical	——— clearance
cheviot	————— · clearing-house

—————	clergyman	—————	commissioner
————	clerkship	————	commitment
.. ..	clerical	———	committee
———	clog	——	commodious
..	codicil	——— ...	commodity
....	coffer	—————	commonly
..	cognizance		communicate
—	coin	————	communication
	coke	....	community
	collapse		company
—	collateral	—— ..	comparatively
—.—	collection	—...	compare
—————	Colorado	.—.	comparing
.— ———	combination	————	comparison
	commence	———.. _	compatibility
	commencement	——	compel
	commerce		compensate
_	commercially	—— _	compensation
_	commissary		competency
..	commission		competent

___ . ___ competition	_ confirming
___ ___ competitors	.___ . conformity
. compilation	. . . . congregation
complete	. . Connecticut
compliance	connecting
component	_ connection
compromised	_ consanguinity
comptroller	_ conscience
compulsion	.___ _ conscientious
computation	___ conscious
___ . ___ . concern	.___ . consecutive
concession	consequence
___ . ˉ _ concurrence	.___ consequently
___ . _ condemnation	___ consideration
. conference	___ _ consignee
_ . _ conferred	___ consignment
___ . ___ confidence	_____ consignor
_____ confidentially	. ___ consistent
_____ confirm	_____ consistently
_____ confirmation	___ . _ conspiracy

———	constituents	———	contributory
———	constructive	———	controvert
———	consul	———	convenience
———	consular	———	convenient
———	consummate	———	conveniently
———	contentious	———	conventionalities
———	contract	———	conveyance
———	contingency	———	cooperage
———	contingent	———	co-operate
———	continental	———	co-operation
———	continuance	———	copartnership
———	continuing	———	cordage
———	continuity	———	cordial
———	continuous	———	corduroy
———	contraband	———	corporal
———	contractor	———	corporation
———	contradict	———	corporeal
———	contrary	———	co-respondent
———	contribute	———	correctness
———	contribution	———	correspondent

	correspondence	· critical
·	council	—— criticise
—	councilor	—·— cross-bar
——	counsel	———— cross-bill
	counselor	—— cross-examination
—··	countenance	—— crude
—··	counterfeit	—— cultivator
	countermand	—·· cumulative
	counterplea	—— currency
	countersign	custodian
— —·	coupon	—— customary
··	court	——— custom-house
·	courtesy	——— —— cylinder
	covenant	
—	crated	——— Dakota
—·	creation	—— damage
———	credential	——— dangerous
———	creditor	——— dealer
———	criminal	——— · debatable
——— ·	· crinoline	———·— debenture

——	debited	————	definitely
———	debtor	———	defray
———	deceased	———	Delaware
———	decide	———	delegate
———	decidedly	—	delinquency
—	decision	———	deliverance
——	declaration	———	demandant
—-	decree	———	demonstrative
——	dedication	———	demurrage
——-	dedimus	——	demurrer
————	deduction	———	denial
———	defalcation	——	denomination
———	defalcator	———	depose
——-	defamation	———	deposit
———	defaulter	———	depositor
——	defeasance	———	depreciate
——-	defendant	————	depreciation
———	deferred	———	derelict
———	deficiency	———	derivative
———	deficient	———	describe

—	description	——	dimension
— -	descripture	·· ···	diphthong
—·	desirable	——·	director
—··	desirous	——	disability
—	desist	- —··	disadvantage
	desperately		disagreeable
-	destination	——·	disappear
	detached	—·—·	disappoint
· detail		——	disappointment
-	determine	—·	disburse
	deterred		disbursement
	deviation		discharging
—⁀·-	device	—··	disciple
·——— devisee		···— ·· disclaimer
- ·· —— diacritical		···· discommode
—·· difference		——— discontinuance
——— different		——— discontinue
——·· differential		——— discovery
——— dignity		——— discrepancy
——— dilapidation		———··· discretion

————— discriminate

————— disencumber

———— dishonest

———— dishonor

——— disinclined

— disinterested

—— —— dispatch

———— dispelled

——— disposal

—— disposition

— — dispute

—— dissimilar

— dissipated

— dissolution

... dissolved

—— distance

———— distinguish

———— distribution

———— disturbance

. —— dividend

——— diverted

———— dockage

——— doctor

- — document

———— documentary

— —— —— domestic

—— double-head

——— drainage

——— drawback

——— drawee

———— drawer

———— draw-head

——— drayage

——— dubious

duplicate

——— duration

———— die

——— dye (color)

——— dyeing

— dying

———·——— earliest

——— easement

———·· eccentric

———— - economy

——— efficacious

— educate

··—··—— ejection

—— ejectment

——·· electric

—— electrical

—·—·· electrotype

—··· elevator

———— eliminated

——·——·· elsewhere

—·· emancipation

··—— embargo

———·—·· embarrass

————— embezzle

————— embezzlement

— ——··- embossed

——— embrace

—·———— embroidered

——— emergency

—— — · emigrant

———··—— emissary

———··· empanel

—— employee

——— emporium

———— empties

·——· empty

———— · enclosure

·——— - encounter

——· ··· encourage

endeavor

——·· endeavoring

—— – endorsement

—— – endowment

——— · energetic

———— · enfranchisement

———— engagement

	engross		especially
	en masse	—— .. _	essential
	ennui	——..	establish
	enormous	——	estate
	enterprise	——	estimate
	entertainment	——...	estoppel
	entitle	—— _	etiquette
	entrance	—..	European
	enunciate	——	eventually
	envelope	—	eviction
_	equalize	——	evidence
——	equally	—	evidently
—	equipment	—.	exacting
—	equitable	——	exactness
——	equivalent	—	exceedingly
	erasing	—..	exceptionable
——	erection	——	exceptionably
——	erroneous	——.	excessively
—	escaping	——...	exchange
——	escheat	————	exchequer

——— exclusively

——— executive

——— executor

——— executory

——— executrix

— exemplification

· exemplary

—· ·——· exercise

—— -—— exhaust

———· - exhibit

——— – *ex officio*

——·—— exorable

——— exorbitant

———·—— *ex parte*

—— — ·—— expenditure

—— ·· - expense

——·—— explanation

——·—— export

——— exposure

——— express

7

——— expunge

——— expurge

— ··· extension

—— extracture

——·· extravagance

——··· extremely

·——· – eyelet

——— - facilitate

——— facilities

——— · facility

——— fastidious

——··· faultless

——··· favorable

——· · feasibility

——··· February

——— felony

——··· fidelity

——— fiduciary

——— – filiation

finance

financial

financier

fireplace

firm

fixture

flannels

Florida

fluctuate

fluctuation

fluid

forbearance

foreclose

foreclosure

foregoing

foreign

forfeit

forgery

forgetful

formerly

fortnight

fortunate

fractional

franchise

frankly

fraudulent

freight

Friday

friendship

frieze

frontage

frontier

fulfilled

fulness

furniture

furrow

furtherance

galvanize

gamble

——————— gambol (frolic)

——————— garnishment

——————— gaseous

——————— gauze

——————— gear

——————— generally

——————— generating

——————— generosity

——————— generous

——————— genuineness

——————— geographical

——————— Georgia

——————— gladsome

——————— glycerine

——————— government

——————— gradually

——————— grantee

——————— grantor

——————— gratified

——————— gravity

——————— grievance

——————— grocery

——————— gross

——————— guage

——————— guarantee

——————— guaranty

——————— guardian

——————— guidance

——————— *habeas corpus*

——————— habitual

——————— handsome

——————— hand-writing

——————— harass

——————— hardware

——————— harmony

——————— harrow

——————— hazardous

——————— heifers

——————— heirloom

———— hereby	— ··· ·— Idaho
———— hereditament	———— identify
———— hereunto	———— ignorance
———— hesitate	———— illegal
——·—— hexagon	———— illegitimate
—— ·· hinged	———— Illinois
—·—— ·— hitherto	———— illustrate
———— hoister	———·— illustration
———·— holographic	———— imaginary
———·— homestead	———— immaterial
——— hominy	———— immediately
——— horizontal	———— impeachment
——·— hostility	———— impertinence
——— Housatonic	——— impious
———— · householder	——— implement
——— ·· humorously	——— implicit
——— · hyphen	——— imply
——·— hypothecate	——— import
———— hypothecation	——— important
	———— impossibility

—— impossible	—— ·· ——· inconsistent
———— impression	———— inconvenience
———— imprimis	———— incorporation
· imprisonment	———·· incorrect
—— · — improvement	———— incumbent
—— impugn	———— incumbered
———· — ·· impunity	———— incumbrance
—· inability	———— incurable
·—· · inaccuracy	———— indebtedness
——·· ··—— inadequacy	·——— indefeasible
— —— inadmissible	·—· indefinite
———·—· inadvertence	——·· indemnify
———— inattention	— · indemnifying
——·· incapable	—— indemnity
———— inception	———— indenture
———· — inchoate	———·· independent
———·· incidental	——— Indiana
——— — incompatible	—·· ·—· Indianapolis
———— incompetent	— ·— indict (charge)
———— inconsiderable	——— indicting

——— indictment   ——— inference

——— indirectly   ——— inferior

— indispensable   ——— infringement

— indite (compose)   ——— ingredient

— inditing   ——— inherit

individual   ——— initials

——— individualism   ——— injunction

——— individually   ——— innocence

——— indorsee   ——— innocent

——— indorsement   ——— innocently

— indorser   ——— innuendo

——— induce   ——— inquiry

——— inducement   ——— insensible

——— industrial   ——— insignificant

— industrious   ——— *in situ*

——— inexorable   ——— insolvency

——— infallible   ——— insolvent

——— infamous   ——— inspection

——— infancy   ——— installment

——— infer   ——— institute

—	instruct		interrupt
—	insufficient	—	intersecting
——	insupportable	-	interceding
——	insurable		interspersed
—	insurance	——	interstate
	intact	———	intervening
—	integrity	———	interview
—	intelligence	———	inthrall
—	intelligent	———	intimate
—	intelligently	———	intolerable
——	intemperance	———	intoxicating
———	interchange	———	introduction
——	interfere	———	invariably
—	interior	———	invitation
——	interlocutor	—	inventory
——	interlocutory	—	investigation
———	intermural	———	investment
———	international	———	investor
———	interplea	—	invoice
———	interrogatory	———	involuntary

——————— Iowa   —— judgment

————.—— irksome   —————. judicial

————————— irksomeness   ———————-— juices

——————— irregularity   ——-——— junction

——————— irrelevant   —— jurisdiction

——————.— irresponsible   ——— jurisprudence

——— irrevocable   ——— juryman

———.— —— issuable   ——————-. justice

——   — issue   ——————-—— justify

———— — . item   ——————— jute

——-.   itemize

                                 ——— Kansas

—————.— jelly   ——— Kentucky

——— ——— jeopardize   ——— knowledge

——— Jersey

——— — jointly   ——————— laborer

——— ...— jointure   ——————-.— lavender

——— —— joist   ———————.. leakage

——— —- journalist   ——————-. lease

——— ...— joyful   ———————-. legacy

—	legatee	.. —.	lottery
—	legislature	—	Louisiana
—.	legitimate	—	lucre
—	. lessee	—	luggage
—.	levy	——	lunatic
—..	liability		
———	libel	——	magistrate
——— . — .	liberal	——	magnanimous
—	librarian	——	Maine
.—	lien	——	maintain
—..	lighter	——— —	malleable
	lighterage	——— .	mammon
——	limitation	——	manacle
—	lineal	——	management
—	linoleum	——	manager
	liquidate	—— — .	mandamus
—	literature	—— —	manifest
—	litigation	—— —	manilla
.—	locomotive	——	manipulation
———	loss	—— .	manipulator

——	manufactory	————	memorial
————	manufacturer	— —	mercantile
————	margin	————	mercenary
——— ——	maritime	——— —	merchandise
——— ——	marriage	————	merit
——— ·——	Maryland	————	meritorious
————	Massachusetts	——— —	method
————	materially	——— ·	metropolitan
——— ——	maturity	——— —	Michigan
————	mayor		microphone
————	meantime	— —	mileage
——— —	meanwhile	————	military
——— ———	mechanic	————	militia
——— ···	mechanical	————	millinery
————	mechanism	————	millionaire
——— ··	medication	————	minimum
—	medicine	————	Minnesota
	Mediterranean	————	minor
—·	membership	· ——·——	minute
————	memorandum	·· —	miscarried

miscellaneous	----	Muskingum
---- misdemeanor	...	muslin
---- misinformed	.----	mutilate
---- Mississippi	------	mutually
Missouri		
misunderstanding	...	narrow
misunderstood	------	naturalization
model	------	Nebraska
modicum	-------	necessarily
moiré	-------	necessary
molasses	-------	necessitate
Monday	---------	necessity
monomania	-------	neglect
- monopolist	-------	negligence
monopoly	-------	negotiable
Montana	------- .	negotiate
. moreover	----------	negotiating
-- -- mortality	--------- .	neighborhood
mortgage	--------	neutral
mundane	... --	Nevada

—	nevertheless	—— . _	number
.._	New Hampshire	——.	nuncupative
—	New Jersey	——	nutrient
—.	New Mexico	——	nutritive
—	New York		
—	niche	——.	obedient
...—	nickel	——	objectionable
	nitrogenous	——	obligation
——.	nominal	—— .._	obligatory
——	non-arrival	——	obviate
—	non-exception	—— .	occasion
—	_ non-delivery	——	occupancy
——	non-joinder	——	occupation
—— . .	non-resident	—	occupy
——— . .	North Carolina	—	occurrence
—————	northwestern	—	officially
———— _	notification	. ——— ..	oftener
——.	nourishment	—— .	Ohio
—	notwithstanding	—— .	Oklahoma
—	nuisance	.—	onerous

— operating	— — . oversight	
— operator	——— . ownership	
opinion		
opportunity	——— Pacific express	
— opulence	——— - pamphlet	
orbit	——— panel	
orchestra	——— pantaloons	
—. — ordinance	——— papal	
—— ordinary	——— paragraphing	
——. . Oregon	——— parallel	
—— organism	——— paramount	
——. ornamental	. —— paraphernalia	
——. ornamentation	—— parcel	
——— — oscillate	.— . —- parenthesis	
——. —. ostrich	—— —. parentheses (plural)	
——— otherwise	——. parquette	
———— outlawry	——— partially	
——— outright	—— particular	
———— outstanding	—— partition	
——— overrule	——. partner	

—	partnership	————	perforate
— —	passage	————	performance
————	passenger	————	period
————	patent	————	perishable
— —	patron	————	perjury
———	payable	————	permission
———	payee	————	perpetual
— ———	payer	————	perplexed
——— —	peculiar	——— —	personal
——— —	pecuniary	——	personally
——— —	pedestal	—— —	perspective
————	penalty	—— —	persuade
—	pendant	————	pertain
——	penknife	————	perusal
—— —	Pennsylvania	———	petition
—	pension	————	petitioner
	per annum	————	petit jury
—	*per capita*	———	petit larceny
—	percentage	— —	petroleum
	peremptory		Philadelphia

phrase		practically
physician		preamble
pier		precedence
Pierrepont		precedent
pipe		precisely
pistol		predecessor
placard		predict
plaintiff		preference
pleasing		prejudice
pledge		premises
plentiful		premium
policy		preponderance
politeness		prescribe
political		presence
pomatum		preservation
pneumatic		previously
porcelain		*prima facie*
possession		principal (chief)
post-mortem		principally
power of attorney		principle (rule)

prior	——— promptness
priority	——— promulgate
privilege	———— propelling
probably	——— property
_ probability	——— proportion
_ probity	——— proportionate
——— _ proceeds	——— propose
——— process	——— proposition
——— — procession	——— propound
——— ——— producer	——— proprietary
——————— proficient	——— proprietor
——————— profile	——— _ *pro rata*
——— — progressing	——— prosecution
——— · prohibit	——— prosperity
· ·· — prohibition	——— prosperous
·— · projection	——— protect
_ prominent	——— protest
——— · promiscuously	——— proverbially
——— promissory note	——— · proviso
——————— promote	——— · provision

—— ... proximity	— ... *quo warranto*
—— publication	
—— publicly	—— random
—— puncheon	—— rascality
—— punctual	—— ratification
—— punctuality	—— ratify
—— punctuate	—— rattan
—— ... purchasable	—— rattling
—— purchaser	—— reaction
—— purporting	—— readjuster
—— purposes	—— real estate
—— pursuant	—— realizing
	—— rear
—— qualified fee	—— reasonable
—— qualify	—— reassurance
—— quantity	—— rebate
—— quarantine	—— receipt
—— quitclaim	—— receiptor
—— quiz	—— receivable
—— quorum	—— receive

8

———— receiver   ———— re-enclose

———— reciprocate   ———— referee

———— recitation   ———— reference

———— recklessly   ———— referring

———— reclamation   ———— refresh

———— recommend   ———— refrigerator

———— recommendation   ———— refund

—— ——— recompense   ———— register

—   recognizance   ———— regretting

—   . recognize   ———— regulation

—— — recognizing   ———— rehearsing

———— recollection   ———— reimburse

———— reconciliation   ———— rein

—— —— reconsider   ———— reinstate

—— - recrimination   —— relationship

—— —— rectify   ———— relegated

———— redeemable   ———— reliability

——— — redemption   —— reliable

——— redirect   ———— reliableness

———— redundantly   ———— religious

relinquish	respectfully
reluctantly	respectively
reminiscence	respondent
remittance	responsible
remuneration	responsibility
renewal	restitution
renunciation	restoration
repetition	restriction
replacing	retirement
replevin	retribution
representation	returnable
representative	revenue
reprimand	reversible
repugnant	revocation
requisite	revolution
requisition	re-written
reservation	Rhode Island
reshipment	ribbed
resource	ribbon
respectability	rode

___	rougher	_____ _	scope
___ __	rubbish	____	screening
_____ _	rumor	_____	sealed
		_____	seaworthiness
____	sacrifice	_____	secrecy
_____ __	salable	_____	secretary
_____ _	salary	_____	section
_____ _ __	salesman	____	security
_____	sanitary	_____	seduction
_____	Saratoga	_____	seizable
_____	sateen	_____	semi-annual
_____ __	satisfactory	_____	*semi-tontine*
_____ __	Saturday	_____	sensitive
___ __	sausage	_____ _	separation
___	scaffolding	_____	separator
_____ _	scarcely	_____	serge
_____	scene	_____	serial
_____ _	schedule	_____	seriously
_____	scheme	_____	serviceable
___ _	scientific	_ ___	sewer

_____ shedder	_____ slovenly
_____ . sheriff	_ _ slyest
_____ Shetland	_____ social
_____ shilling	_____ . society
___ ___ .. shipment	_____ .. sole
shorthand	_____ _ solicitation
shrewdly	_____ ... soliciting
... shrinkage	_____ ... solicitor
_____ .. _ shrivel	_ _____ .. solvent
_____ *sic semper tyrannis*	_ _ _ somebody
_____ side-bar	_____ sometimes
_____ signature	_____ ... somewhat
_____ Silesia	_____ _ South Carolina
_____ similar	.. ___ .... southeastern
_____ .. singeing	_____ . specific
___ ___. singing	_____. specification
___ ___ situated	_____ _ specimen
_____ skein	_____ speedily
_____ skilful	_____ spelter
_____ skull	_____ spirituous

spurious	structure
stability	subordinate
statistics	subpœna
statuary	subrogation
statue	subscribe
statu quo	subscription
statute	subsequent
statutory	subsequently
stenographer	substance
steward	substantially
stiffening	substantiate
stimulating	substitute
stipend	subterfuge
stipulate	suburban
stipulation	success
stockholder	successor
stockyard	successful
stoppage	sufferance
storekeeper	sufficient
strengthen	suitable

suite	———	systematic
summarily		
summons		tallow
Sunday	—	tapestry
superintendence		tariff
superintendent		technicality
superior	.. -	telegram
supersede	— —..	telegraph
supersedeas	— ..	telephone
supervision	...	temporarily
supplemental	——..	tendency
surety	-——... .—	Tennessee
surmise	——...	terminate
surrender	——— -	territorial
surveyorship	—	territory
suspension	———	testamentary
swindler	———	testator
switched	———. —	testatrix
switchman	———	testimonial
syndicate	——...	testimony

_____ Texas	_____ __ transaction
_____ texture	_____ transcribe
_____ therefor	transferable
_____ therefore	- ___ transferred
_____ thereon	___ transferring
thereto	_ _ _ transit
_____ thoroughly	____ transmission
_____ Thursday	____ transmit
_____ throat	_____ transportation
_____ throughout	_____ traveller
_____ tierce	_____ treacherous
_____ tissue	_____ treasurer
_____ tolerable	_____ trespass
____ tolerate	___ _ _ _ trestle
_ ____ tonnage	_____ tribunal
_____ tontine	_____ tribute
_____ touching	_____ triplicate
_____ to wit	_____ troches
_____ township	_____ trustees
_____ traffic	_____ trustworthy

Tuesday		unconsciously
- tunnel	—	undecipherable
turbine	——	undeniably
typewriter	——	undenied
typewriting	—	underscoring
typewritist	——.	undergo
	——. ..	undersigned
ultimatum	——.	understanding
unaccompanied	_ . -	undivided
unambiguous	.	undertaking
unanimity		undoubtedly
unassorted		unexpectedly
— unattainable	_	unexpired
unauthorize	.	unfavorable
unavoidable	—	unforeseen
unbleached	—— --	unfolding
- uncancelled	——	unfortunate
- uncertain	.——	ungranted
- uncoagulated	——--	unhesitatingly
uncollectible	——	unimportant

	unimproved	--	upholster
— -- --	United States	—	— upright
—	unload	— —	upwards
—	unmistakable	—	urgent
	unmounted		useless
-	unnecessary		usually
-	unpardonable	—	usurious
	unpleasant	- -	Utah
	unprofitable		
-	unquestionable		vacancy
	unreasonable	–	Valencia raisins
	unreliable	- -	validity
	unremitting	—	valuable
	unrouted	—	value
	unshaken		valve
	unsuccessful	–	variance
	unsupport	— —	vegetable
— -	untroubled	—	vendee
———	unusual	———	vendor
———	unwarranted	——— -	ventilation

veracity		waive
verdict		warehouse
Vermont		warrant
vessel		warrantee
vexation		warrantor
vibrating		warranty deed
vice versa		Washington Territory
victorious		Wednesday
view		weighmaster
vintage		West Virginia
Virginia		whatsoever
vitality		whenever
vitalize		whereabouts
voidable		whereof
volume		whereupon
voluminous		whiffle-tree
voluntarily		whiskey
voluntary		wholesale
volunteer		wiring
voucher		Wisconsin

—	withdrawn	———— Wyoming
—	withhold	
—	witnesseth	———— yielding
-	worsted	
	wrap	————zeal

COMPOUND WORDS.

This is a much-vexed question, and the dictionaries now in use are so inconsistent with themselves that they are not safe guides. Many words of various endings are written as one word if the compound makes only two syllables, but with a hyphen if of more than two. Many prefer to use the hyphen in some cases where the rules would dispense with it ; and of course its use is a matter of taste, as much as of custom. Wherever any doubt would arise as to the meaning of a compound phrase, the hyphen should be used. The following directions (mainly selected from Bigelow's *Handbook of Punctuation*) may assist in making this matter clearer, if not exhaustive of the subject :

Military and civil titles, such as the following, are compounded : Governor-general, attorney-general, lieutenant-colonel, rear-admiral, vice-president, etc. ; *but* viceroy and vicegerent.

The following words denoting *kindred* are compounded : Father-in-law, etc., step-mother, etc., foster-brother, etc., half-sister, etc., cousin-german, second-cousin, grand-uncle, great-aunt, great-grandfather, etc.

The following *points of the compass* should be written as single words : Northeast, northwest, southeast, southwest ; *but* north-northeast, south-southwest, etc.

Compounds of *half* or *quarter*, such as the following, are always printed with a hyphen : Half-dollar, half-crown, half-barrel, half-past, half-way, half-witted, half-yearly, half-price, quarter-barrel, quarter-day, quarter-deck, quarter-face, etc. : *but* quartermaster.

The words *fold, score, penny*, and *pence*, united with numbers of one syllable, are written as single words ; but with numbers of more than one syllable they are compounded or written separately : Tenfold, twenty-fold, a hundred-fold, two hundred-fold ; fourscore, twenty score, a hundred score ; halfpenny, twopenny, halfpence, fourpence, fifteen-penny, fifteen pence, etc.

Numerals of one syllable compounded with various words, and *ordinal numbers* compounded with *hand* and *rate*, are commonly written with a hyphen ; for example : One eyed, two-story, four-footed, etc. ; second-hand, first-rate, etc. Numerals are also compounded with nouns to form adjectives, as one-horse chaise, two-foot rule, sixteen-foot pole, etc.

Compounds ending with *holder, monger, man, woman* and *work* are usually written as single words, unless the combination is unusual ; for example : Shareholder, bondholder ; ironmonger, scandalmonger ; Dutchman, workingman, fisherman ; Irishwoman, needlewoman, saleswoman ; groundwork, needlework, stonework, etc. ; *but* mason-work and carpenter-work.

Compounds ending with *boat, book, drop, house, light, room, side,* or *yard,* are made single words if the first part of the compound is of only one syllable, but are joined by a hyphen if more than one ; for example : Rowboat, steamboat, canalboat, ferry-boat ; handbook, bankbook, daybook, commonplace-book ; dewdrop, raindrop, waterdrop ; alehouse, bathhouse, warehouse, dwellinghouse, summer-house ; candle-light, daylight, lamplight ; bedroom, ante-room, dining-room, dressing-room ; fireside, hillside, mountain-side, riverside ; churchyard, farmyard, stable-yard, lumberyard, marble-yard, etc.

Compounds ending with *like* are written as single words, unless unusual combinations, or derived from a proper noun, when they are written with a hyphen ; for example : Workmanlike, manlike, womanlike, lifelike ; miniature-like, business-like, Arab-like, Satan-like, etc.

NOTE.

The writer wishes to acknowledge his indebtedness to that capital work, *Humphrey's Manual*, for most of the illustrative examples used in this work.

www.ingramcontent.com/pod-product-compliance
Lightning Source LLC
Chambersburg PA
CBHW030607270326
41927CB00007B/1085